Robert Ekin M'Bride

In the Ranks

From the Wilderness to Appomattox Court House

Robert Ekin M'Bride

In the Ranks

From the Wilderness to Appomattox Court House

ISBN/EAN: 9783337133627

Printed in Europe, USA, Canada, Australia, Japan

Cover: Foto ©ninafisch / pixelio.de

More available books at **www.hansebooks.com**

R. E. McBRIDE.

FROM THE

Wilderness to Appomattox Court-House.

THE WAR,

AS SEEN AND EXPERIENCED BY A PRIVATE SOLDIER IN THE ARMY OF THE POTOMAC.

By REV. R. E. M'BRIDE.

A tale of the times of old. The deeds of days of other years.
—Ossian.

CINCINNATI:
PRINTED BY WALDEN & STOWE,
FOR THE AUTHOR.
1881

Entered, according to Act of Congress, in the year 1881, by

R. E. M'BRIDE,

In the Office of the Librarian of Congress, at Washington.

PREFACE.

IN giving this book to the public we do so under the same plea which justifies those pleasant gatherings called "reunions," where men of the same regiment, corps, or army, meet to extend friendly greetings to each other, to friends, and all comrades in arms.

The writer has found it a pleasant task to recall the scenes of fifteen years ago, when, a mere boy in years, he had a part in the events here recorded. He is conscious of a kindly affection toward the men who were his companions during those stirring times. Kindness, thoughtfulness, forbearance, toward the boy-soldier, are not forgotten. If he found any thing different from these in his intercourse with men or officers, it has passed from memory, and he would not recall it if he could.

We trust, also, that this work may have a mission of utility to the generation that has grown up since the war.

There is a certain almost indefinable something, which has been summed up under the expression, "military traditions." This comes not alone from formal histories of the wars of the nation, but more largely from the history which each soldier carried home with him after the war was over. It meant something more than a certain amount of small family vanity, when men used to say, "My father was a soldier of the Revolution;" "My father fought at Lundy's Lane."

There lay back of this the stories told to wondering little ones while they gathered around the arm-chair of the soldier grandfather. Here were planted the seeds of military ardor that found expression at Gettysburg, Vicksburg, Atlanta, and the Wilderness. It is thus the past of the nation projects itself into the present. Our comrades that sleep down yonder guard their country more effectually than if, full armed, they kept unceasing watch on all her borders. Though dead, they yet speak,—yes *live*, in the spirit which yet lives in the hearts of their countrymen. The cause they died for our children will love; the institutions they preserved at such cost, our sons will perpetuate by intelligent devotion to freedom and her laws.

Is it in vain, then, my comrade, that I sit down in your family circle, and tell your children the story of our hardships, trials, reverses, victories?

This narrative is submitted to you almost as first written, when intended only for the perusal of my own family. In recounting events subsequent to August 19, 1864, when the One Hundred and Ninetieth is spoken of, the One Hundred and Ninety-first is also included, as they were practically one.

Since completing the work, the author has learned that the report of the Adjutant-general of Pennsylvania gives these regiments, the One Hundred and Ninetieth and One Hundred and Ninety-first, no credit for service subsequent to the battle of Welden Railroad, in

August, 1864. We give an explanation of this in the closing chapter, and send forth this volume, hoping that it may serve, in some measure, to do justice to as devoted a body of men as Pennsylvania sent to the field.

SENECA, KANSAS, March, 1881.

CONTENTS.

	PAGE.
ALEXANDER, JOHN,	25
Appomattox Battle,	215
Amusements,	93, 158
BETHSAIDA CHURCH,	66
Birkman, Capt.,	72, 118
Boggs, Lieut.,	35
Baiers, Lieut.,	21
CARLE, COL.,	94, 100, 225
Coleman, Mike,	26, 68, 172, 182
Coleman, Sergt.,	47, 72
Culp, Eckard,	68
Craig, Wm.,	39
DELO, CHAPLAIN,	59
Dodds, Jasper,	21
Dunn, Geo.,	134
Dillinger,	121
ESHELMAN, ABE,	26, 85
Elliot, John,	28
Execution,	133
Edgar, John,	170

	PAGE.
FORT FEDERAL HILL,	112
Fort Steadman,	162
Five Forks Battle,	188
GAINES' MILL BATTLE,	20
Ginter,	217
Ghosts,	49
Graham, Daniel,	60
Gravelly Run Battle,	172
Grossman, Louis,	40
HARRIS, WM.,	135
Hatcher's Run Battle,	148
Hartshorn,	73
Hayden, Lieut.,	73, 221
Hop,	135
JONES, CAPT.,	31
KINSEY, CAPT.,	73, 120
Kenedy, W. H. H.,	224
M'CULLOUGH, M. F.,	31
M'Guire, J.,	135
Miller, Ed.,	182
Moreland, C. L.,	63, 100
Mortars,	88
Mushrush, Benj.,	27
NORTH ANN RIVER BATTLE,	62
OVERDOFF,	120

Contents.

	PAGE.
PETERSBURG,	85
Pattee, Col.,	73, 85, 118, 179, 219
Peacock, Lieut.,	118
Preston, Geo.,	121
QUAKER ROAD BATTLE,	171
ROBBINS,	215
Rowanty Creek Battle,	148
Running the Gauntlet,	90
Rutter, Wm.,	85
Ramrods,	93
STANLEY, JOHN,	31, 69
Stewart, Joe,	25
Stewart, Capt.,	22
Steen, David,	33
Shaffer, J.,	68
Spottsylvania,	37
WALB, L. C.,	204
Welden Railroad,	118
Welden Raid,	124
White, Allen,	31
White Oak Swamp Battle,	75
Wilderness Battle,	30
Woods, O'Harra,	22
Wright, Ernest,	218
Whisky,	140

INTRODUCTION.

I HAVE long purposed the following work, designing to put in a form somewhat permanent my recollections of experiences in the great war, believing it may be a source of satisfaction to my children in later years. Already many of those scenes begin to appear dim and dreamlike, through the receding years, and many faces, once so clearly pictured in memory as seen around the camp-fire, in the march, and on the field of battle, have faded quite away. These things admonish me that what is done must be done quickly.

In the following pages you will find the names of men otherwise unknown, because their part in the great conflict was an humble one, yet none the less grand and heroic. This is written during the brief and uncertain intervals of leisure that may be caught up here and there amid the pressing work of the pastorate. You will not, then, I trust, undervalue it because of literary blemishes. It is *history* as really as more pretentious works. It is a specimen of the *minutiæ* of history, a story of the war as seen by a private in the ranks, not by one who, as a favored spectator, could survey the movements of a whole army at a glance, and hence could, *must*, individualize brigades, divisions, army corps. It is the war in field, woods, underbrush, picket-post, skirmish-line, camp, march, bivouac. During 1864 no memorandum was kept, and a diary kept during the spring of 1865 was lost, within a year after the close of the war. Hence I have depended on memory alone, aided in fixing dates, etc., by reference to written works. Beyond this, the histories consulted were of little assistance, as their record of events sometimes differed materially from my recollection of them. In such cases I tell my own story, as the object is to record these things as they appeared to me.

In recording events of which I was not myself a witness, I give the story as heard from the lips of comrades. Such portions are easily discernible in the body of the narrative. You can have them for what they are worth.

> "I can not tell how the truth may be,
> I tell the tale as 't was told to me."

In the Ranks.

Chapter I.

"WAR!"

IT is a little word. A child may pronounce it; but what word that ever fell from human lips has a meaning full of such intensity of horror as this little word? At its sound there rises up a grim vision of "confused noise and garments rolled in blood." April 12, 1861, cannon fired by traitor hands, boomed out over Charleston harbor. The dire sound that shook the air that Spring morning did not die away in reverberating echoes from sea to shore, from island to headland. It rolled on through all the land, over mountain and valley, moaning in every home, at every fireside, "War! War! War!"

Are we a civilized people? What is civilization? Is it possible to eliminate the tiger from human nature? Who would have dreamed that the men of the North, busy with plowing and sowing, planning, contriving, inventing, could prove themselves on a hundred battle-fields a fiercely warlike people? The world looked on with wonder as they rushed eagerly into the conflict, pouring out their blood like water and their wealth without measure, for a sentiment, a principle, that may be summed up in the one word—"nationality." "The great uprising" was not the movement of a blind, unreasoning impulse. A fire had been smoldering in the North for years. The first cannon shot, that hurtled around the old flag as it floated over the walls of Fort Sumter shook down the barriers that confined it, and the free winds of liberty fanned it to a devouring flame.

The Yankee—let the name be proudly spoken—as he turned the furrow, stood by his work bench, or listened to the jarring clank of his machinery, had mused with heavy heart and shame-flushed cheek how a haughty, brutal, un-American spirit had drawn a line across the land, and said, "Beyond this is *not* your country. Here your free speech, free labor, and free thought shall never come." While this line was imaginary, he had waited for better days and larger thought to change the current of the times; but when it was transformed into bristling bayonets and frowning cannon, the tiger rose up within him, and with unquestioning faith he took up the gauge of battle. Men talked of the "cold blood of the North." That blood had surged impetuously through the veins of warrior freemen for a hundred generations. Here in the New World it had lost none of its vigor. The sturdy spirit that in other years ruled the hand that wielded the battle-ax, still ruled, when the hand was employed in subduing mountain and prairie. The North was averse to war, because it was rising to that higher civilization that abhors violence, discards brute methods, and relies on the intellectual and moral. Such a people, driven to desperation, move right forward to the accomplishment of their object with a scorn of cost or consequences unknown to a lower type. Hence it is that the people of the North, without hesitation, grappled with a rebellion the most formidable ever successfully encountered by any government. For a like reason their great armies, melting away like frost before the sun when the rebel flag went down, mingled again with the people without jar or confusion.

Turning away from a half million graves, wherein they had buried their slain, their bravest and best beloved, they forgot all bitterness for joy that peace had come. No people in the world had greater reason for severity than the victors in this strife. War, willful, unprovoked, without the shadow of justification, had been thrust upon them. This had been preceded by a series of usurpations the most unblushing ever endured by a free people. These were a part of the plan of a band of traitors, who had plotted for years to overthrow the existing order of things, and establish an empire with human slavery for its chief corner-stone.

The "Golden Circle," with its center at Havana, Cuba, its radii extending to Pennsylvania on the North, the isthmus on the south, and sweeping from shore to shore, was the bold dream of the men who plotted the destruction of the American republic. Their object was pursued with a cold-blooded disregard of all right, human and divine, worthy of the pagan brutality of the Roman Triumvirate. Prating about the "Constitution" with hypocritical cant, they trampled upon every safeguard of popular liberty, and at last, in defiance of even the forms of law, plunged the people of the Southern States into a war with the government, which, even if successful in securing a separation, could only have been the beginning of woes, as their plans would develop.

But notwithstanding the heinousness of the accomplished crime, not a man was punished. It is doubtful whether popular opinion would have approved the punishment of even the arch-traitor, Jeff Davis. The common sentiment was expressed by the oft-repeated verdict: "Enough of blood has been shed." Whether this was wise or not it is vain to inquire. Perhaps the future will vindicate the wisdom of the generous course of the government. Thus far it has seemed like folly. The South has shown a persistent vindictiveness unequaled in the history of any people, a cruelty toward the helpless victims of their hate that is shameful to the last degree. The cowardly assassination of political opponents, the brutal murder of black men, women, and children, has been defended openly or covertly by pulpit, press, and platform. If any disapprove, their voice is not heard in condemnation of the wrong.

This may have resulted partly from the fact that many of the people of the North, notably many so-called statesmen, ignored common sense and gave way to gush and sentiment. There is nothing gained in this prosy world by calling black white. The leaders of the rebellion were guilty of the horrible crime of *treason*, and we baptized it something else. The result is manifest to all who are not willfully and wickedly blind to the facts.

Yet it is the part of duty to hope for the speedy coming of an era of calmer judgment, of real and healthy patriotism, when every American citizen will claim our whole land as his *country*.

Chapter II.

WHEN the civil war began, my home was with the family of Mr. John Dunn, in Butler County, Pennsylvania. The old gentleman was a Democrat, and at first had little to say about the war. One evening he returned from the village in a state of intense excitement. He had heard of the disastrous battle at Bull Run. It is no exaggeration to say that he "pranced" around the room, chewing his tobacco with great vigor, telling how many of our "poor boys" had been slaughtered by the —— rebels. His apathy was at an end. He could see where the line lay between treason and patriotism, when once that line was traced in blood.

At this time two Butler County companies, C and D, of the Eleventh Pennsylvania Reserve Volunteer Corps, were in camp near Pittsburg. The corps was sent forward to Washington at once, and from that time till the close of their term of service, they gallantly represented the Keystone State in every battle fought by the Army of the Potomac. My brother, Wm. A., was a private in Company C. He enlisted June 10, 1861, and fell, with many other brave men, at the battle of Gaines' Mill, June 27, 1862.

From what I could learn from those who were present, the following are the facts concerning the disaster which befell the regiment in this engagement, and my brother's death:

Late in the afternoon of the 27th, the Eleventh moved forward to relieve a New Jersey regiment, which had been fighting in a piece of woods near the center of the line. The rebels came swarming against them, line after line, but were continually driven back by the relentless volleys that blazed out from the ranks of the Eleventh. Unfortunately, about the time they became engaged, the line on either side of them was driven back, and they were left to contend alone against terrible odds. Neither men nor officers knew their real situation until men began to fall, from volleys poured into them from the flanks. Major Johns went in the direction from which the fire was coming, thinking that some of our own troops were firing on them through mistake. He was made prisoner. Adjutant

M'Coy was ordered to report the condition of things to General Mead. On reaching the open ground, he saw the battle flags of nine rebel regiments on the flank and rear. He at once reported to the colonel. Orders were given to fall back, the intention being to hew a way out through the enemy. At this point my brother fell. Having just loaded his gun as the command was given to move toward the rear, he paused to give a parting shot. A bullet struck him in the face, penetrating the brain, and he fell dead.

The regiment, hemmed in on every side by overwhelming numbers, with one-fourth of their number killed or wounded, at last surrendered. Company D lost eight men, killed, in this engagement, besides a number mortally wounded or permanently disabled. Of the former was Jasper Dodds, who was wounded in the knee by a rifle ball. After being removed to Richmond, he wrote a cheerful letter to his mother and friends at home, no doubt expecting to recover. He died July 18th. Jacob Baiers, then sergeant, afterwards promoted to captain, was shot through the lungs, and never wholly recovered. He continued in service, however, until April, 1864.

The regiment was exchanged in time to participate in the second Bull Run battle, where again their loss was terrible. Seven men of Company D were killed or mortally wounded. It is said that Jesse Fry and Boss. M'Cullough were the only men of the company on their feet and unhurt at the close of the battle. Scarcely were their ranks somewhat filled up by returning convalescents, when the other great battles followed. On every field they left their dead. "South Mountain," "Antietam," "Fredericksburg,"—these words you can see in the muster roll, after that word which even yet chills the heart, "killed." Captain Stewart was struck through the breast at Fredericksburg, and died in two hours. Young O'Harra Woods was promoted for gallant conduct in this battle. The honor was well bestowed and nobly borne. He fell at Gettysburg, July 2, 1863, bravely leading his men in that great battle. But why particularize; brave men all.

> "Theirs not to make reply,
> Theirs not to reason why,
> Theirs but to do and die."

Chapter III.

BUTLER COUNTY, famous for rocks, hills, buckwheat, psalm-singing, and soap mines. Psalm singing? Yes. The sturdy Scotch-Irish that grew among her hills, as a rule, would sing to the Lord with no other words than those of the warrior king and the holy men of old. Have you heard their solemn songs? I hear them to-night—it is not imagination, not "their songs," but "our songs." A voice of singing floats down through the years, very holy and very tender; for now all the singers are "evermore before the throne," except two, whose infant lips could scarce pronounce the words:

"Lord, bless and pity us,
　Shine on us with thy face;
That th' earth thy way, and nations all
　May know thy saving grace."

Yes, psalm-singing! But the soap mines? We protest! We have hunted huckleberries on her hills; we have pursued the ground-hog in her woods, the 'coon around her cornfields; we have swum and fished in her sparkling streams; from Dan to Beersheba we have worked, played, done "many things we ought not to have done," and left undone many things it was our duty to do; but we never saw a soap mine. We can testify before all the world that the people of Butler County make their soap in the usual innocent and odorous manner.

PROSPECT, Butler County, a dreamy village of the olden time. The houses accommodate themselves to the cross-roads. One road stretches from the county seat westward; the other from the "stone house" goes winding along toward Pittsburg. The houses have also a contented, self satisfied look; the stores and the tavern seem to consider themselves permanent factors in the world's machinery. On a pleasant day an "honorable" or two might be seen sunning themselves in front of store or tavern, whittling, and adding dignity to the surroundings.

In this quiet village one chilly morning in December, 1863, the writer mounted the stage-coach and went rattling over the frozen ground toward Pittsburg, to enlist in the volunteer service. Just seventeen years ago that very morning I had begun the business of life on rather limited capital; and although it had been improved with considerable success, yet the kindly prophecies, particularly of my copperhead friends, did not portend a very lengthy nor brilliant military career. The next day I made my way to the provost-marshal's office, and, after due examination, was pronounced all right, and sworn into the service. If I lied about my age, obliging memory has written it over with something else, and it is gone from me. But I think Captain ——, of Prospect, did the lying; at least let us hope that he has sufficiently repented of it long ere this.

I selected Company D, of the Eleventh Pennsylvania Regular Volunteer Corps, and was assigned accordingly. The recruits were retained for some time at Camp Copeland, then about the dreariest, most uncomfortable place I ever saw; shelter and provisions insufficient, bad whisky and blacklegs abundant. Joe Stewart, John Alexander, and myself tented together here. They had enlisted for the One Hundredth Pennsylvania, the "Roundheads." Joe was an old acquaintance. He served gallantly till the close of the war.

John was a noble boy and found a soldier's death at Cold Harbor. After one of the fruitless charges made there, when the Roundheads came back foiled of their purpose, John was not with them. In the darkness of night which quickly closed around, Joe went out to search for him. As he was picking his way steathily among the dead and dying, he heard a well known voice calling softly near by, "Joe, Joe, is that you?" It was John, lying there, shot through the breast. He warned his rescuer to be very cautious, as the rebel videttes were near. With much difficulty he got him back to our lines. This was the night of June 2d, and he died on the 4th.

I left the latter part of January to join the regiment, then camped at Bristor Station, on the Orange and Alexandria Railroad. With me were two recruits for Company E, Abe Eshelman and Mike Coleman. The former was killed at Petersburg; the latter, a live Irishman, was mustered out at the close of the war, after a year and a half of valiant service for his adopted country. We went by Harrisburg, Baltimore, and Washington, thence by the Orange and Alexandria road, every mile historic ground, past Bull Run, where, the soldiers say, the dead would not stay buried, and finally we alight at Bristor Station. On the right over there are the Bucktails; a little further toward the west the Second is camped. Over the hill toward Brentsville, past the artillery camp, is the Eleventh.

Here I found John Elliot, who had served with the regiment since its organization. He, brother William, and myself had been boy companions before the war, although I was younger than they. I went into the mess with him, S. L. Parker, and Benjamin Mushrush. After being with them but a short time, I was taken with that scourge of the army, measles, and was removed to the surgeon's tent. I was on picket when the disease made itself felt. The day and night on which I was on duty were stormy, rain and snow. As a result, I had a lively time of it. The disease left my voice so impaired that, for a long time, I was unable to speak above a whisper. During my stay at the surgeon's tent, I employed myself studying his books on surgery, and acquired a knowledge on the subject which was utilized at a later period.

John Elliot had enlisted April 25, 1861, although not mustered into the United States service until July 5th of the same year. He felt that he should be mustered out at the former date of 1864. As the time drew near we conversed frequently on the subject, and he was in some perplexity as to duty in the case. The morning of the 25th found him on picket. I prepared the morning meal for the mess and then relieved him until he should breakfast. Soon he returned in a more than usually cheerful spirit. After chatting pleasantly for a time, he spoke of his term of enlistment.

"I have that matter all arranged now," he said, "as far as I am concerned. I am not certain whether the government has a right to hold me any longer or not; but I will stay till it sees fit to discharge me. The country needs soldiers this Spring. I would like to visit home. It's been three years since I saw mother and the boys; but it's all right. God has kept me safely through all these battles, and I can trust him for time to come."

This was the substance of his language, his exact words, as near as I can remember. They are noble words; as grand as ever fell from the lips of Christian hero. Many a time afterward they were an inspiration to me. His face was bright that beautiful Spring morning with a joy that was not of earth. The night watches had been spent communing with God,—yes, face to face. Had he known that the midsummer sun would look down upon his grave, would his decision have been different? I think not. He knew too much of war and battles not to count the cost. From a Southern prison-pen his brave spirit went up to God.

Chapter IV.

APRIL 29th we broke camp and proceeded to near Culpepper Court-house. Before leaving camp we sent our extra baggage, clothing, etc., to Washington, and, of course, never saw them again. During the night of May 3d we marched for the Rapidan, crossing at Germania Ford. The next evening we camped in order of battle near the Wilderness Tavern. The following morning the division moved out on a country road toward Robertson's Tavern. Passing through woods, we came to an open field, where line of battle was formed. The Bucktails were in front, skirmishing. We could see them on the ridge, and their occasional shouts and rapid firing showed that the battle had begun. For the first time I heard the whistle of the rifle ball, as a stray one now and then whistled over the line of battle. After waiting thus for some time, we moved back some distance, in the direction from which we had come. Here I spoke a few words with John Elliot, the last we ever exchanged. In the confusion which followed he was made prisoner, and died at Andersonville. Soon the noise of battle began to deepen in our front and at the right. Hurried orders were received; the line moved by the right flank, double-quick. The Seventh Regiment deployed and vanished into the woods, forward, and the Eleventh followed in line of battle. Moving on through the thick underbrush, the enemy was quickly encountered. Their first volley was deadly. A ball struck Boss. M'Cullough in the forehead. He fell dead, a portion of his shattered brain lodging on the arm of John Stanley, a boy of seventeen, who had come to us during the Spring. John shuddered, shook it from the sleeve of his blouse, raised his gun and began firing. Captain Jones, of Company A, White, of Company C, and many others, fell dead before this first volley. Soon it was discovered that the division was flanked. Our line was at right angles with the position in which the subsequent fighting took place. To crown all, the woods took fire, and soon the only problem that remained was to withdraw as quickly and safely as possible.

While this turmoil was progressing, to me so strange and bewildering, the surgeon, Dr. Lyon, came across me, and directed me to go to a certain point at the edge of the woods, east of the Wilderness Tavern, to help care for the wounded. Thither I made my way. As I passed on through the woods, I was soon out of reach of the bullets, which had been flying thick and fast. When I came to the open ground, I saw more clearly than ever the results of the battle, still going on in the woods beyond. The multitude of wounded and dying men crowded the road. Some were limping painfully along; others were being carried on stretchers, or helped along by comrades.

Reaching the designated place, I found the field tents erected, and all full of suffering men. I took charge of one in which were twenty-seven wounded, several amputations, and other bad cases. They lay with their heads toward the canvas, a narrow path being left between their feet. All that could be done for them was to give them food and water, bathe their wounds, and render any little service by which their sufferings might be mitigated. Their heroic patience astonished me. Men, torn and mangled, would utter no groan, nor give any vocal expression to the agonies which racked them, except sometimes when sleep or delirium found the overmastering will off guard.

Toward evening I learned that the regiment was just beyond the Wilderness tavern; and, getting relieved for a short time, I started to go to them, as I had the extra coffee of the mess. As I came in sight, they moved hurriedly away toward the right, where the battle was raging fiercely. It was useless to follow, and I began to retrace my steps. Pausing a moment on an elevated knoll, I gazed on the strange scene that spread out before me. From the right on the turnpike, a line, somewhat curved, extended a distance of three or four miles to the left. On the right the line was enveloped in woods, in which a terrific conflict was going on. Sedgwick's corps was standing between the army and disaster. In the center, on elevated ground, beyond some low woods, I could see a rebel line of battle, while the sharp fire of skirmishers in front showed that here the lines of blue and gray would soon smite together. Further toward the left, a line of blue extended along the edge of a narrow field, facing the woods just beyond, into which it poured incessant volleys, while the smoke that rose up from the woods showed that an active foe was there. Behind our line, flat on the ground, lay a second one. A tragedy, grandly, awfully sublime, was enacting before me. A hundred thousand men were grappling in deadly conflict. While I gazed the line of battle slackened its fire; the second one rose from the ground; then both swept forward across the field and into the woods beyond, bearing the enemy before them. For a few moments there was silence, and then the struggle was renewed as fiercely as ever. I returned to the field-tents to go on with my work of mercy among the suffering.

As night drew on the battle ceased, and the men lay down to sleep where they had fought, ready to renew the strife at the return of light. In the tents there, while the army beyond was resting, part of our nation's heroes continued the contest through the solemn hours of night. They fought with the giant Pain, and some of them went down into the dark valley, and close by the chill waters they faced the King of Terrors.

I slept none that night. As morning approached, I went to the edge of the little opening which had been cleared in the woods for the tents. While I stood here looking off toward the scene of yesterday's battle, the sound of a single rifle shot rang out on the air, then another and another, and then a deafening roar of musketry burst forth and raged along the whole line, continuing almost without interruption all day.

In the afternoon Lieutenant Boggs and David Steen were brought in wounded, the former by a rifle ball in the thigh, the latter severely bruised by a fragment of shell. He had been wounded at Gaines' Mill and Fredericksburg. After his return this time, I heard him say that he had come to have more dread of going into battle since he had been wounded so often. Still he never shrank from duty. He was killed the following August at Welden Railroad.

Here I saw the only instance of impatience on the part of a wounded man of which I have any recollection. A young fellow lay about the middle of the tent, wounded in the knee, a ball having cut the skin on one side without injuring the bone.

His long legs were extended almost across the narrow path along which I was compelled to walk in passing from one to another. He was grumbling and complaining, demanding and receiving attentions in a gruff and uncivil manner. He would also mutter threatenings of what he would do should I hurt him in stepping over his crooked legs outstretched in my way. To all of this I paid no attention and signs of ill-nature continued. Finally, a bright young man opposite, whose leg was amputated at the thigh, raised himself on his elbow and proceeded to express his opinion of such conduct in language much more forcible than pious.

From this place we moved some distance to the left, where the tents were erected in an open field. Here an incident occurred which illustrates the false estimate placed upon the civilization of the North by the masses of the South. A wounded rebel, an intelligent-looking young man, was brought in from the field in an ambulance. We came with a stretcher to carry him into the tent. He looked at us with a frightened, helpless look, and asked:

"You won't hurt me, will you?"

I assured him we would be just as careful

as possible. He seemed surprised to be treated with kindness, having been taught, evidently, that the Yankee invader was a barbarian. Removed to the tent, I examined his wound. A bullet had passed through the ankle joint, and the only remedy was amputation. He inquired how it was. It seemed hard to tell him that he must go through life maimed.

"That is a bad foot; but the surgeons will do the best they can for it. You may lose it." Some time after he was removed, I suppose to have his foot amputated, and I saw him no more.

The next move was to Spottsylvania. Grant had grappled with his enemy, intending to hold on "all Summer." The same spirit seemed to animate his army, from General Meade down to the latest recruit in the ranks. The lines of blue came out from the smoking underbrush of the Wilderness, their ranks torn and decimated, and closed in around the bristling batteries and rifle-pits of Spottsylvania with a relentless courage that was sublime.

Here the tents were pitched in a little, open lot, a house to the right as you faced the position where the fighting was in progress. The tents were not sufficient to contain the wounded, and they lay on the ground on the outside by thousands. Those long rows of suffering forms, gashed and mangled in every conceivable manner, told a dreadful tale of human wrath. That gallant division, the Reserves, had preserved their well-earned reputation for stubborn valor at a terrible cost. Their greatest loss was sustained in a single onset against the rebel position. The enemy was posted in strong rifle-pits, beyond a narrow strip of swamp. Orders were given to charge these works. The division moved forward. They had never failed in such an undertaking. Their charge had always pierced the enemy's line. This had been their record during three years of warfare. But men can not accomplish impossibilities. Baffled by the swamp, cut by the merciless fire that blazed out from the pits, they are driven back, rally, re-form and charge the second and third time, and then retire to the position from which they had come out.

The field-tents here were nearer the front than before. Bullets and an occasional shell whistled over us. My work was still the same, caring for the wounded, assisting the surgeon, or occasionally binding up a wound myself.

During the second day, while engaged at the farther end of the tent, I heard at the front a familiar voice. As soon as I was disengaged I went to the front end of the tent, eager to learn from whom the well-known voice proceeded. There lay a large, noble-looking young man, severely wounded in the thigh. He was conversing quietly with a wounded comrade by his side. Voice and face were as familiar as if heard and seen but yesterday. Puzzled and deeply interested, I did not speak, but proceeded to bathe his wound. While thus engaged, his eyes fell upon my face. Looking at me intently a moment, his face brightened, and he exclaimed:

"You are Rob M'Bride, are n't you?"

"Yes; and you are Billy Craig," was the immediate reply.

As soon as he pronounced my name, it all came to me in a moment. We had been school-mates at Courtney's School-house. He was then one of the "big boys," and I a lad of nine or ten. I had not seen him since. He was one of those large-hearted, royal souls, that could find pleasure in little acts of kindness, that bound me to him very closely. He bore his sufferings with heroic fortitude. When the time came to remove the wounded, and they were being hurried away in ambulances and rough army wagons, I went to Dr. Lyon and told him of the case. He went with me to an ambulance and ordered room reserved in it for him. I then had him carried to it, made him as comfortable as possible, bade him good-bye and God speed, and saw him no more on earth. He died from his wound some time in June.

May 11th, Lewis Grossman, of Company C, was brought in, terribly wounded by a shell. One arm and leg were crushed, and he was otherwise bruised. I did not see him until after the arm and leg were amputated. He was a young man of great physical endurance, or he would never have rallied from the shock. He was as pale as a corpse when first brought into the tent, but rallied in a little while, and was able to take some refreshment. When left to himself his mind wandered, and he would talk as if he were engaged in the quiet pursuits of peace. Unless prevented, he would remove the bandages from the stumps of his amputated limbs. When spoken to, however, he would refrain from this, and talk rationally of the present circumstances. Dr. Lyon finally told me to give my attention entirely to him. This I did until he was sent away. He told me how his wound was received. He was in front, skirmishing. He was in the road in front of a rebel battery, and in the act of loading his gun. Perceiving they were about to fire, he still delayed a moment, thinking to get in another shot before leaping to the shelter of a large tree that stood near. It was a costly delay.

The shell came screaming toward him, burst, and dashed him stunned and mangled to the ground. As he concluded this narrative, he added, with the utmost seriousness: "But they have n't made much off me, after all. I 've peppered them in almost every battle the Potomac army has fought since the war began."

He got along finely, and there seemed every prospect of recovery. When some of the boys called on him at Washington, on their way home in June, he requested them to say nothing to his friends about the extent of his wounds. But from some cause—perhaps gangrene—he died August 3d, and is buried in the National Cemetery at Arlington.

Nearly opposite Lewis lay a young man of very fine face and attractive appearance. He was mortally wounded. Most of the time his sufferings were very great, but no earthly skill could bring any relief. As death drew on, his mind wandered. He was fighting his battles over again. He was not the poor, crushed mortality that lay here. His spirit was over yonder, where the cannon's sullen roar and the awful din of musketry, the cheers of the struggling combatants, told of a deadly strife. Sometimes he was distressed and troubled, sometimes exultant. Anon his face would light up with the strange fire of battle, and he would raise his arm and cheer. Once he said quite distinctly: "Here is a chance for a brave man." Later he became calm, and quietly fell asleep, to wake no more on earth till the great day of God.

> "Soldier, sleep, thy warfare o'er,
>   Sleep the sleep that knows no waking,
>   Dream of battle-fields no more."

One of the Bucktail Regiment lay on the ground in front of the tent, shot through the chest. He was, perhaps, twenty-five years of age, large and well-formed, his face stamped with the marks of intelligence. While engaged near him, I saw another of that band of heroes coming toward him with great strides, an expression of anguish on his face which I can not forget. He threw himself on his knees by the wounded man, kissed him, then covered his face with his hands, and his great manly form shook with convulsive sobbings. Tears trickled down the cheeks of the other. Not a word was spoken until, after a while, the storm of emotion had passed. Then they conversed calmly for a while, and parted with the quiet dignity of brave men who say farewell while the shadow of death lies dark around them.

A man was brought in shot through both thighs. I did not know his name, but had heard his voice among the worshipers in the church-tent at Bristoe Station, and knew that he was a man of God. After a brief examination, the surgeon announced that amputation would be necessary.

"Very well, doctor; get around to it as quick as you can. I suffer terribly."

Another was shot in the thigh, the bone shattered to the hip. When told that the limb must be amputated he objected.

"But you will die if it is not done."

"I can't help that; it shall not be amputated with my consent."

Within twenty-four hours he was dead. Whether wise in his decision or not, he met the result without flinching or complaint.

A boy with his arm torn off by a shell expressed his only complaint in the words, "I never can fight any more."

One evening, worn out by constant labor and watching, I lay down in a vacant place in the tent, from which a dead soldier had been removed, to find rest for mind and body in sleep. As I lay there thinking of the dreadful scenes around me, of the wounded and dying here, the dead just over yonder, I began to wonder what would be the sensations of a man shot in the brain. Suddenly there came a shock, as if the whole machinery of life had stopped at once. How long a time elapsed before consciousness was resumed I do not know; the interval may have been momentary; but as a dim sense of being stole over me again, I was quite convinced that a stray shot had struck me in the head. Rousing myself, I deliberately felt my head, to learn the exact state of things. To my surprise and gratification, I found every thing in due order. I leave it to those who are skilled in the mysteries of the nervous system to explain the phenomenon; but you must allow me to believe that I know something of what it is to be shot in the head.

The time arrived, at length, when the field hospitals must be moved because of the changed position of the army. A heavy rain began on the 11th, and continued for some days, making the roads almost impassable. The wounded that remained were removed as speedily and as mercifully as possible. Some had to be left behind. Nurses were detailed to remain with them. As night came on every thing was in readiness, and the rest of us were directed to take our departure without delay. Two of us started together after dark. We made our way through the mud and intense darkness about twenty rods, to the edge of a wood. We resolved to go no further, come what might. Doubling myself up at the root of an old stump, I was soon oblivious to both rain and danger. Just as day was breaking, I awoke, and arousing my companion, we hastened away.

Chapter V.

THIS closed my experience in the hospital. I was so worn out by the constant strain which such labor made on body and mind, that rest was imperative. During all these days I could get no definite information of the fate of John Elliot. The wounded reported that he was missing, but whether among the dead or living they could not tell. It was difficult to drive away the thought of the painful possibilities that imagination would bring up. Had he been disabled that first day in the wilderness and perished in the flames of the burning woods? Had he been mortally wounded, and died alone in the thick underbrush which veiled so many tragic scenes? Had death come more swiftly and mercifully, or was he a prisoner and unharmed? Such were the questions that might be solved by inquiry among the members of the company.

After some delay I found the regiment by a little stream called the Ny. The spot on which they were camped, or rather resting under arms, was within beautiful shelling range of the rebel batteries, as I found out afterward to my great discomfort and dismay. Toward evening, Sergeant W. Coleman was taken quite sick, and at his request I started with him to find the hospital. After proceeding some distance, he became so ill that we could go no further, and some means of conveyance must be found. A stretcher was procured, and two men to carry him. To these I confided my charge, and began to retrace my steps. It was now after dark, a clear, moonless night. Crossing the little stream at the point where I had left the regiment a few hours before, to my great disappointment not a man could be found.

What to do was a puzzling question. The resolution was finally taken to spend a few hours, at least, in trying to find them. At first I started in a direction bearing toward the right, but soon met a column marching toward the left. Reasoning that if troops were being moved to the left, none would be moving at the same time toward the right, I fell in with this column. determined to see what the outcome would be. Soon the open ground was crossed, and the column began to bear to the right of its line of march, through the woods. Presently I noticed that an unusual silence was observed. Not a word was spoken above a whisper, every noise and clatter incident to the march were carefully avoided.

Growing weary at length, and reflecting that after all I might be going away from the regiment instead of toward it, I dropped out of the line and lay down against the root of a tree close to the road, to sleep till morning. Half sleeping and half waking I lay there, dreamily watching that army of shadows gliding stealthily by. Shadows they seemed as they moved hurriedly along under the gloom of the overhanging trees, as noiseless almost as an army of spirits from Homer's nether world. The mystery of this secret night march served to quicken imagination, and I could see this same column grimly marshaling in "battle's magnificently stern array" in the dim light of the coming morning, ready to burst upon some exposed point of the enemy's line.

Opening my eyes a little later, the same ghostly procession was filing past, but in an opposite direction. This meant that, sooner or later, my rest must be disturbed, or I might be left in an exposed and dangerous position. Present comfort, however, being the stronger motive just then, prevailed, and I sank into unconsciousness again. From this I was aroused by some one shaking me by the shoulder and warning me in a whisper that I must wake up and come on. The muffled "tramp, tramp" had ceased, the rear of that shadowy army was vanishing in the darkness; one solitary figure waited, delaying a moment, to see if I was fully awake. Rising, I followed. Reaching the open ground from which we had entered the woods, I found myself alone and bewildered. Proceeding some distance with rather a vague notion of direction, I determined to make a final halt till morning. All that was necessary to make myself comfortable was to sink down on the ground without removing any thing, my knapsack fitting conveniently under the back of my head, supporting head and shoulder as if intended for the purpose. Thus bestowing myself by the side of a rail fence, I was soon sleeping soundly.

But my rest was destined not to be undisturbed. Something awoke me. What! Was this night given over to ghosts and spirits intangible? Again the forms of men were gliding noiselessly about me. Above were the twinkling stars, around were busy men, and silence everywhere. With instinctive cautiousness I lay motionless, furtively noting the curious scene. A moment's careful attention explained it in part. One by one the rails of the fence were taken up with the utmost caution and borne away. They were building breastworks somewhere. There was work to be done, I thought, and preferred to finish my much delayed sleep, if allowed to do so. I lay motionless, only sufficiently awake to dimly take in the situation. Twice men came and stooped over me with their faces close to mine, looked intently, and turned away in silence. Congratulating myself on my good fortune, that I was going to sleep the night out while others worked, I gave myself again to repose.

When I awoke the sun had got fairly started on his course, and was pouring his rays full into my face. The events of the preceding night seemed like a dream; but there was evidence about me that my visitants had not been as ghostly as they seemed. The fence by which I had lain down had disappeared, and I was alone in an open field. Utterly bewildered, I addressed myself to the somewhat difficult task of deciding what must be done. On either side of me could be seen what I knew to be earth-works, but not a living thing was visible. The field gave evidence of having been fought over, for the well-known *débris* of a battle were strewn around. At length my mind was made up to go to the rear, find the division hospital, and get information.

But where *was* rear? Where was front? Where was any thing? After meditating profoundly on these questions, I decided that my course lay in the direction of the earth-works on one side of the open ground. This was the "rear," and these works had been abandoned in the progress of advance. Proceeding leisurely in this direction, I had not advanced far until I was surprised by the boom of a cannon behind me. A shell screamed over my head, and exploded with a sharp ring against the earth-works a few hundred yards ahead of me. Looking back, I saw a Yankee officer standing on the earth-work, glass in hand, watching the effects of the shot. This was a revelation. I was between the lines, and heading for the rebel works. That shot saved me a trip to a Confederate prison-pen. Hastily retracing my steps, I lost no time in reaching our lines, expecting each moment that an artillery battle would break out while I was between the combatants. The position was perhaps a half-mile to the right of the spot where I had last seen the regiment. No infantry was visible, but no doubt there were troops concealed in the woods near by. The sharp ridges by which the open ground was broken were occupied by artillery, the men standing by their guns.

The day was before me, and I was resolved to have a little more experience; the more so as I could make my observations in comparative safety. Those guns frowning grimly over the earthern redoubts meant mischief. I would see an artillery fight; my curiosity was soon amply gratified. Standing near a vacant redoubt, looking toward the rebel batteries, suddenly a white smoke burst forth, followed by the roar of cannon and the hissing shriek of shells, as the noisy missiles came tearing through the air toward us. After the first discharge, the rebel fire was directed chiefly to the right of the earth-work behind which I had taken refuge, though shells kept striking and bursting around. My position, however, was favorable for a view of our own batteries, and for observing the effect of the enemy's fire. Sometimes the shells would strike the ground, sending the dirt many feet into the air, and go tearing across the field, touching the ground and bounding again at intervals. Others would strike the earth-works, or explode in the air, and hurl their fragments far and near, whizzing and buzzing to the earth.

This noisy combat lasted for some time, and ceased,—not because either of the combatants was seriously damaged, as far as I could see, but because they were tired of it.

This will be as appropriate a place as any to remark, that "shelling" is usually quite harmless, except when the guns are served by skilled artillerists, and under favorable circumstances. Unless the shell is exploded at the proper distance and altitude in front of a line, it is not likely to do any injury. A cannonade which, to the uninitiated, would seem sufficient to destroy every thing before it, will be faced with the utmost equanimity by veteran troops, if the artillerist have the range too "long." It is always very annoying, however, as there is no telling when a shell may prove a little "short," and distribute its fragments for rods along the line. The men are usually ordered to lie down, unless directly engaged. The shell cleaves the air with a frightful sound, that is but faintly described by the word "shriek." Few men can refrain from "dodging," as the dangerous missile comes over with its unearthly sound. The writer has frequently tried it, but can remember no instance of marked success, except while engaged, or otherwise employed. Perhaps the most disagreeable sound of all, is when the guns are charged with grape and cannister, and send their destructive contents through the air with a grinding, groaning, gnashing sound, that chills the blood of the listener. This may partly result from association, as such a charge is seldom used except at close range, on a charging line. Then, if directed by cool, determined men, the effect is terrible. Those who have once heard this sound can never forget it. It requires but little imagination to fancy that the fiend which was sending forth such loud defiance just now, has grappled with his adversary and is hissing out his horrid rage in the midst of Titanic strugglings. A little experience will enable you to determine from the sound what a gun is firing; shot, shell, or grape. The artillerymen usually have little fear of shell, but dread a volley from infantry. With the infantry the case is reversed. Generally the men preferred the branch of service to which they were accustomed. Each did not envy the other.

The cavalryman rode all day; but at night he had to care for both himself and horse. The infantryman had nothing to care for but himself. He would make his coffee, and sleep all night, while the cavalryman must scout, or picket front or flank. Sometimes the infantry must spend a part of the night in throwing up breastworks, or making a night march; but usually he considers himself more certain of rest and comfort than his fellow-soldiers of the mounted force.

Chapter VI.

I NOW continued my search for information as to the whereabouts of the regiment. I had almost reached the little flat by the Ny, at the point where I had last seen my comrades the evening before, when, to my astonishment, the roar of cannon broke forth again, and the shells came hissing over my head and bursting all around me. There was not even a stump or stone for shelter from the pelting storm of iron, and in the woods just over the stream, the trees were being torn and rent asunder as if by thunderbolts. This was more of a joke than I had bargained for. Reflecting a moment, I concluded to take my chances among the trees. A slender foot-log over the stream afforded means of crossing. When about the middle of the log a shell howled close to my head and dashed through a tree with a fearful crash. Nothing deterred, I sat down at the root of a sturdy oak which would shelter me from fragments, at least, and waited for something to "turn up." The rebels evidently thought that troops were concealed in the woods, and were determined to make it hot for them. They made it lively for me; but unless that afforded them some satisfaction, they might have saved their ammunition.

Later I learned that the Reserves had moved to the left. Passing along in that direction, I came to a hill on which a battery was planted. The men were standing by their guns, ready for action. Close behind these, on the face of the hill were the caissons, and back of these, men holding the horses, the men themselves sheltered in holes which they had dug in the hillside. Things looked decidedly breezy about that hill. My curiosity to witness an artillery fight had been fully gratified some time before; so I passed on without delay, and soon found the object of my search some distance further to the left.

Late in the afternoon of the 17th an orderly galloped to headquarters, the bugle sounded "fall in," and we were moving toward the right at a rapid pace. Heavy firing could be heard in the direction of our right flank, and we were hurrying toward the scene of action, to strengthen the threatened point. We arrived about dark. The fighting had almost ceased, and the enemy were handsomely repulsed. The attack had been made on a body of inexperienced troops, mostly heavy artillery, who were marching from Fredericksburg to join the Army of the Potomac. They were well-drilled and disciplined, and made a gallant and successful fight, though with heavy loss. In their first fight they had faced Lee's best veterans, and defeated them. The old soldiers were inclined to regard it as rather a joke—the lively manner in which the rebs welcomed them to the front. This disposition to see a bright, a laughable side to every thing, may be set down as one of the peculiarities of the Yankee soldier. In victory or defeat, success or disaster, ease or hardship, some one of a group of soldiers could find something from which to extract a jest or on which to found a pun.

The next morning I went out over the field. Details of men were engaged in burying their fallen comrades. The dead were collected in groups, a trench sufficiently wide and deep was dug, and they were laid side by side as decently as possible, and covered with two or three feet of earth. When it could be done, the graves were marked. I have seen this done by our men for the rebel dead, when there was time and leisure for such care.

Under an apple tree lay a rebel who had been shot in the forehead, a little above the center. He must have been shot before sunset of the previous day. It was about noon when I saw him, and strange to say, he was still alive. He was unconscious, and probably had been from the moment he was struck.

In a negro cabin lay a young rebel soldier, a fair-faced, handsome boy, shot through the right lung. I inquired after his wants, and made him as comfortable as might be. He said he had not suffered for want of care. Soldiers had been in frequently during the day, and all had been very kind. He spoke of this with great satisfaction. I notified Dr. Lyon of the case, and he was taken care of.

The next day we advanced some distance toward the enemy. Skirmishers were thrown forward, but no serious fighting took place. As the skirmishers were going out, Chaplain Delo dryly inquired if he might not accompany them, 'giving as his reason that he would like to get Captain Coder's horse killed if it could be done conveniently. He had charge of a horse belonging to the captain, who had displeased him about something in connection with the horse. There was no opportunity of gratifying the worthy chaplain's wishes.

Again the army was in motion, leaving behind now as useless what before had been fought for so tenaciously. As we moved away, the Eleventh was in the rear, nothing between us and the enemy, but some cavalry, to cover the rear of the column, as the army moved off to strike Lee from a new position. We were passing over a wide, open piece of country. The rebel cavalry and our own had become hotly engaged, and a spirited fight was in progress clear across the open ground behind us.

About this time Daniel Graham became quite ill, and was compelled to fall out of the ranks. I remained with him to help him along. The undertaking proved to be rather a serious one. He would struggle bravely on for a while, and then sit down panting and exhausted. I carried his gun and knapsack, and finally took him by the arm to keep him up.

Meantime the battle going on behind us

drew nearer and nearer, and the bullets were whistling around us with uncomfortable frequency. At last Daniel became utterly discouraged; and, as he dropped upon the ground to rest at one of his frequent halts, he declared it was no use, he could go no further. He urged me to leave him, and make my escape.

"There's no use of talking that way. After you rest a few minutes, we'll try it again."

"But I'm clear used up, and there's no use of both of us being prisoners."

"We're not prisoners yet by a good deal. We are going to come out all right. You are worth two dead men yet."

But notwithstanding my brave words, I was almost of his opinion, though not convinced that the time had come to give up all hope. It was my duty to stay with him as long as there was any prospect of getting him off.

Our cavalry was now nearly up to where we were, and I announced that he must come along. Helping him to his feet, we started. Courage and strength now seemed to revive. We made good progress, and were soon out of danger. In the course of an hour or two he was able to take his gun again, and in the evening we came up with the regiment.

In trying to recall the scenes of this period, there are some that seem like the fragments of a half-forgotten dream, distinct in themselves, but without any definite connection as to time or place. They are but pictures, some of them becoming faded and indistinct; others bright and fresh, as if they had come from the painter's hand but yesterday. I see a long column of weary soldiers, winding along over hill and valley, in the night, gliding past a stately mansion, with beautiful grounds and shaded walks, and every-where the freshness and fragrance of Spring. Again I see a line of battle stretching out across an open field, the men resting lazily in their ranks. A little to the left, near some shade trees, stands a battery, ready for action, the guns pointing toward some unseen enemy beyond. It is noon, and the sunlight is pouring down upon the scene, bright and clear.

May 23d we came to the North Ann. We halted in open ground, before we reached the river. Fighting was in progress at the front, where the rebels were disputing the passage of the river. While we waited here, a battery came thundering past at full speed, and soon the roar of their guns told that they had found something to do.

While this was in progress, we were ordered to move. The column was headed, first to the rear, then toward our right. By a rapid march we reached a ford, higher up the river. Without delay we waded right through. The water was swift, and three or four feet deep in places. The bottom of the river was stony, and the stones were slippery. This, with the swiftness of the stream, made the footing of the most active rather precarious. A German, named Moreland, a teacher by profession, and a man of fine qualities, had joined the company but a little while before. He was not very active at best, and at this time had very sore feet. As we were hurrying across, suddenly a wonderful splashing and floundering were heard toward the rear of the company, and Moreland's feet were discovered twinkling above the surface of the water, while with his head he seemed to be making a critical examination of the bottom of the stream. At last he regained his footing, puffing and blowing like a porpoise, amid the cheers and horse-laughs of his comrades.

Once across, no time was to be lost. We had stolen a march on the rebels, and if we would use our advantage we must be about it. The movement was not long unknown to the enemy. As fast as the troops reached the high ground on the other side, they formed line of battle, keeping the left flank covered by the river, and facing down stream. As the remaining troops crossed, they formed on the right, the line as it formed advancing downward and outward from the river, in a curve.

The Eleventh was not far from the left. They moved down the stream some distance, and halted in the midst of a beautiful farm. Before them was a valley, across which the Bucktails were advancing as skirmishers, and beyond this the ground rose again, and curved off toward woods in the distance. Scarcely had our line reached this point, when the enemy "came down like the wolf on the fold." Judging from the promptness and vigor with which they assailed us, they evidently counted on making our enterprise another Ball's Bluff affair.

As the Bucktails advanced, their rapid firing warned us that they had discovered the advance of the enemy. Dust was seen rising on the high ground beyond, and horses were dimly seen. We judged that batteries were coming into position. We were not long in doubt. Suddenly a perfect volley of artillery burst forth. The air seemed filled with the shrieking shells and whizzing fragments. The men could do no more than lie down and let the storm rage. For some time we had not a single gun in position to reply, and the rebels poured in their fire without hindrance. Soldiers who had been through all the battles of the Potomac army, affirmed that they never experienced such a noisy onset, except at Gettysburg. As quickly as possible our batteries came into position, on both sides of the river. Now the tumult was doubled. The earth seemed to shake. When our artillery opened in reply, the rebels turned their attention in that direction; but on account of the awkwardness of their gunners, we were annoyed almost as much as when under their direct fire. On the right there was severe infantry fighting. Of this we could hear little, on account of the terrible cannonading going on around us. The losses of the regiment were slight, owing to the fact that the rebels overshot us. A few were wounded, but I think none were killed. The loss of the corps was about 350. The rebel loss was reported at 1,000, including General Brown, who was in command.

 May was now drawing to a close, and with it would close the history of the Pennsylvania Reserves. The 30th found us in the vicinity of Bethsaida Church. We were moving on with those stops and starts which indicate that the head of the column has met with some obstruction. Skirmishing was going on in front, and from time to time the boom of cannon came rolling up from the left. We were moving along a road which led through open farm country, and through a strip of woods, beyond which skirmishing was heard. During one of the frequent halts, while the men were resting, some standing, others sitting or reclining at ease, a rifle ball came whistling through the air, and struck with a sharp snap in the rail-pile on which myself and others were sitting. It struck between Jim Shaffer and myself. We both naturally squirmed a little at the unpleasant nearness of the malicious little messenger. The affair called forth laughter and jocular exclamations from those around: "How are you *Johnnie!*" "Hit 'em again!" "Go *in!*"

The incident would not have caused any special notice, had it not been so unexpected, on account of our distance from the scene of action.

Forward now through the woods, out upon the open ground beyond, where the division is forming for its last battle. Their left now rests not far from where their right was when they fought at Gaines' Mill, nearly two years before. They advance some distance. "Some one has blundered." They have no support on either wing. They are flanked, and, after a brief struggle, are driven back. Some noble men were lost here. Parks, of Company D, is mortally wounded; Daniel Graham is made prisoner. In the retreat, two men carry back John Stanley, wounded in the arm and side. At the wood they rally. A fence is torn down, and with this and whatever is nearest at hand a breastwork is hastily improvised. A few of the Bucktails have rallied on their right, and thrown up a similar defense of logs, rails, any thing that can stop a bullet. Here the line seems to terminate;

but just beyond and a little back, is a brass battery, concealed by bushes, every gun charged with grape and canister. A house stands close behind the line, in a recess of the woods.

Now the enemy is seen advancing. Line after line comes swinging out. Shells come screaming over. One explodes in front of Company D. Its fragments sever the flagstaff close to Jim Shaffer's head, rip open Mike Coleman's cap, tear off Culp's arm near the shoulder. Another bursts in the house, and sets it on fire. A woman, bearing a baby in one arm and leading by the hand a little child, comes out of the house, still unharmed. Frightened and bewildered, she is passing along the rear of the line instead of hastening away from it. A kind-hearted soldier directs her toward a place of safety. But now the rebel lines are within rifle range. Volley after volley is poured into them, and their ranks melt before the terrible fire. In our front they falter; but toward the right they see a chance for victory. They will swing around our flank, and crush us as they did but an hour before. With exultant yells, their left comes sweeping on, wheeling to envelop our right. But now there bursts from the underbrush a blast as if from the pit, crashing, tearing, grinding, enfilading their lines, leaving in its track a swath of dead and dying. This is decisive, and the battle is won.

Over a hundred dead were counted in front of the Eleventh and the few Bucktails on their right. One man was struck with a charge of grape, or by a bursting shell, and his body from the knees to the neck was crushed and torn into an indistinguishable mass.

John Stanley, who was wounded in this action, was a brave, noble boy. Looking along the company line, with its veterans of so many battles, the remnant of a hundred as brave men as ever followed a battle flag, you would not have guessed that this boyish face could be the calmest in the hour of trial. During that month of battles, he was always in his place, without bravado, but with unflinching courage, doing his duty. I saw him at the woods, as they were taking him from the field. His pale face was as calm as ever. He never returned to us, nor did I learn the result of his wounds.

The next morning the Reserves were withdrawn from the front. Their term of service had expired. The veterans and recruits were reorganized, forming the One Hundred and Ninetieth and One Hundred and Ninety-first Pennsylvania Volunteer Infantry. The others started on their homeward march.

Of Company D, fourteen men returned— five non-commissioned officers and nine privates. Eleven had re-enlisted. Thirty-five were dead, of whom twenty-three had been killed in battle or mortally wounded; and six were prisoners in the hands of the enemy, of whom two died.

Of the eleven veterans, only seven were present, the others being wounded or prisoners. By the close of the war, forty of the original one hundred and one had died in the service. During the first three years, twenty-four were discharged for wounds or sickness. Such is the record of these heroic men. Mingled feelings of joy and sadness were in the hearts of all, as good-byes were spoken, and they marched away. The war-worn veterans, who now turned their footsteps homeward, and those who stood there, watching their going that day, knew too well how certainly these "good-byes" might be "farewells." I think I saw tears in a certain brave colonel's eyes; and perhaps strong hands were clasped with a little more than usual fervor, as friend looked into the face of friend; but there was no "scene." These men were too much in earnest for that.

Chapter VII.

THEN came reorganization. It seemed like a " general breaking up." It was. Instead of the mere handful of men that stood about the torn and tattered colors of the old regiment but yesterday, nearly a thousand were grouped together in the new organization. They might all be considered veterans. Some had been in service since the beginning of the war; all had, at least, the experience of the present campaign. It was generally felt that the new regiment had in it some elements of success not to be found in one brought into existence under ordinary circumstances. The officers of both regiments were tried men, who had the confidence of all. Most of them had risen from the ranks, and had received promotion, step by step, with the approval of their comrades. Sergeant William Coleman, of Company D, was made first-lieutenant of Company I; and Lieutenant R. Birkman, of Company E, was promoted to captain of Company A, of the One Hundred and Ninetieth. These both served faithfully until the close of the war. Lieutenant Hayden, of Company —, of the Eleventh, was transferred to the One Hundred and Ninety-first, and lost a leg at Appomattox Court-house, the morning of Lee's surrender.

With organization still incomplete, these two regiments were pushed forward to the front, and had a share in the terrible fighting at Cold Harbor. As soon as possible, however, the organization was completed, and the two companion regiments became the Third Brigade, Third Division, Fifth Army Corps. William R. Hartshorn was commissioned colonel of the One Hundred and Ninetieth, and Joseph B. Pattee lieutenant-colonel. The latter, a brave and capable officer, commanded the regiment during its entire history, except when absent, wounded, as Colonel Hartshorn was absent, for some cause, most of the time. I was assigned to Company C. Neri B. Kinsey was captain. Lieutenant Moses W. Lucore was in command until some time after July, when Captain Kinsey returned. He was severely wounded, in October, and discharged the following March, on account of his wounds. The regiment adopted the bucktail, in honor of the old "Bucktails," who were more largely represented in the One Hundred and Ninetieth than any other regiment.

In the afternoon of June 12th, we received marching orders, and soon tents were struck, and we were on our way, none knew whither. At this time we were short of provisions. I had a very small quantity of coffee, but nothing else, except fresh meat, which had just been issued. When orders came to strike tents for the march, I was engaged in cooking a slice of fresh beef, by holding it to the fire, spitted on a sharp stick. With an appetite sharpened by a more than orthodox fast, I was watching the operation most devoutly; and the savory odor which rose from the sputtering morsel awakened anticipations which only a ferociously hungry man can imagine. But I was doomed to illustrate the words of the Scottish bard:

> "The best laid plans of mice or men
> Gang aft aglee."

With my half-cooked meat in my hand, I swung on my knapsack, and we marched away. The march continued, without intermission, during the night, except now and then a brief halt for rest. Towards morning we crossed the Chickahominy, at Long's Bridge. Here we halted for rest and breakfast. My entire commissary outfit consisted of about one teaspoonful of coffee. We had halted for breakfast, and might as well go through with the programme. I went to the river and procured about a pint of liquid from that famous stream, and boiled the coffee with due circumspection, and drank the product.

The final member of the above sentence is not inserted to inform the reader that we did not *eat* the "product; but, in explanation, when we thought of that Chickahominy water, the "old man" stirred mightily within us, and we greatly desired to say that it was good, knowing well with what unction every unfortunate that ever tasted it, would say, "O, *what* a lie!" We would like also to insert a few thoughts about G. Washington, who could not tell a lie, but we forbear. We drank that coffee as a war measure.

Our course was then toward the right, a short distance along the river, soon bearing away from it toward Richmond. During the forenoon we reached White Oak Swamp, where the enemy was encountered in strong force. We moved out past some timber to where the cavalry were skirmishing with rebel troops posted in the woods beyond. Part of the regiment deployed as skirmishers and advanced to where the cavalry were fighting and joined in the fray. The rest remained in their rear as support. We lay down in a slight depression of the ground about four rods behind the skirmishers. As we were getting into position a few were wounded; but after arrangements were completed, we lay in comparative safety. About three hundred or more yards to the left, on a little knoll, two guns were in position. Except these, which seemed unsupported, I could see no other force. Where the other troops were or how posted, I have not been able to make out.

The day was warm, and after our night march, the men were fatigued and sleepy. Before long many of them were sleeping soundly, unmindful of the bullets that were whistling over. I do not know how long we lay thus. There is a peculiar satisfaction in sleeping under circumstances of danger. You are no more exposed than when awake, and you don't have to do the thinking. Suddenly I awoke to a consciousness that something had "broken loose." A volley of musketry was poured into us from the rising ground in front of our skirmishers, and the bullets were hissing close above us. I lay still a moment as they passed over, and then sprang to my feet. The skirmishers were giving way, still facing the rebel line of battle that was charging forward. On the left, our guns were belching forth grape and canister into the rebel infantry, that came sweeping on like ocean waves. I think these guns were lost. The last I saw of them the rebel troops seemed to roll right over them. We were driven back to the woods. Here we checked their advance, and held the ground till night. A part of the Fifth Corps and one division of cavalry had been thrown up in this direction to make a diversion, and also to cover the flank of Grant's army while it crossed the Peninsula to the James River, and placed itself before Petersburg. Hence there was not much object in fighting except to hold our position for a sufficient length of time. In the evening a heavy force of the enemy was reported moving toward our left. For this reason, or in carrying out the original programme, we marched in the same direction, starting just after dark. As we fell back in the afternoon, I found a haversack containing some hard-tack. This our mess divided. We did not fail to commiserate the unlucky chap whose loss was our gain. This was a very unsatisfactory fight. It always seemed to me like a scrub race. The rebels plunged in as if they thought it was a 2.20 affair, at the least. The march continued all night. About two in the morning I concluded that the thing had gone on about long enough, and, without any ceremony, made my bed beside a stump in a little opening in a strip of woods through which we were passing. It was after sunrise when I awoke. Breakfast was not an elaborate affair, and was quickly dispatched. It consisted of the vivid recollection of the two delicious hard-tacks which I had eaten the day before. It was light diet, but the best that could be afforded. I found that the column, after keeping the road right on for some time, had about faced and retraced their steps to a point opposite where I had slept. A road here led to the left of our original line of march. This they followed a couple of miles and camped. I found them without trouble.

Here we waited, with nothing to eat, till the evening of the 15th. This is the only time I ever felt the pangs of extreme hunger. During three days and nights of almost constant marching and fighting, I had eaten one ration of fresh beef and two crackers. It seemed as if I was all stomach, and each several cubic inch of that stomach clamoring incessantly for "grub."

The boys amused themselves laying out an imaginary bill of fare. The merits of sundry inviting dishes were zealously discussed. Roast turkey was eloquently extolled by one; another set forth the attractions of a table to which forest, mountain-stream, or river had contributed delights. Sometimes the grotesque imagination of some wild fellow would conjure up a feast so full of horror that a famished cannibal might well protest. In striking contrast with this was the gentle pathos of word and manner as some boy told of dinner at the old farm-house among the hills, where mother poured out the fragrant coffee, rich with honest cream.

NOTE.—Some additional facts have been learned regarding this affair. The One Hundred and Ninety-first was on our left, beyond the battery. The attack was made about four in the afternoon. The One Hundred and Ninety-first had fallen back, and Colonel Pattee had received orders to withdraw. Deeming it hazardous to retire across open ground under such a fire, he rallied the skirmishers on the reserve, and met the charge of the enemy there. In a few minutes the Colonel's horse was shot dead under him. After a sharp fight the rebels broke, and we retreated to the woods before they could rally. The battery was not captured. A failure to hold our position here would have compelled a general battle, and delayed the flank movement to the James.

Chapter VIII.

ON the 16th we marched to the James River. I do not know at what point. The rest of the corps, together with the Second, Sixth, and Ninth, had crossed at Wilcox's Landing. I think we must have reached the river lower down. We were crowded on board transports. Judging from the time we were on board, we must have been carried a considerable distance up the river. We landed on the south side. Here we rested awhile. I went down to the river to bathe and to wash a shirt. Hundreds of soldiers were in the water, plunging, splashing, diving, enjoying themselves like schoolboys. After sharing in the sport to my heart's content, I washed my shirt. The process was simple enough. The garment was well soaped, then held on a large stone and pounded with a club or anything convenient. A final washing out completed the operation. This is the usual *modus operandi* during a campaign. When I have described this process in these latter days, some of my good friends have manifested an unreasonable and unnecessary skepticism as to the real and ultimate object of the pounding. But I solemnly affirm that the purpose is to expel the dirt from the garment.

There is a little animal. Every soldier knows him. Noah Webster, LL.D., knew him. Noah is good authority. He derives his name from the Gothic verb *liusan*, to devour.

The noble Roman knew him. He called him *pediculus*. He is truly democratic in his instincts and disposition.

HE IS A COPPERHEAD.

He loves a rebel. But a copperhead loves a fat army contract. So does he. On this line he is cosmopolitan. He has some splendid business qualifications. He is modest, retiring, persistent, insinuating. He comes to stay. He will stay if you let him. He sticketh closer than a brother. If you don't want him you must skirmish for him. You can not argue him out of it.

I once knew a warrior that cultivated him contrary to army regulations. We protested. They were firm friends, like David and Jonathan.

One day stern Law, embodied in a corporal and a file of men with glistening bayonets, took that man down to the running brook, and, regardless of the frosty air and chilly temperature, with a scrubbing broom they cleansed and variously purified him, furnished him a new outfit of regulation clothing, and brought him back as bright and rosy as need be. He made some remarks. They were comprehensive, but not to edification, and we will not reproduce them. If that veteran still breathes the vital air, he voted for Hancock last Fall.

This seems like a digression, but it is suggested by the facts of the case. As before remarked, I washed that shirt. When I began it was only an ordinary shirt. When I got through it was a most extraordinary garment. There were "millions in it." I skirmished, and washed again. The result was astonishing. I thought of Moses, Aaron, and Egypt, and wondered why Pharaoh did not let the people go. It was a *moving* sight. It may be there yet, or it may have followed the army. I do not know. I retired from the scene sadder, but wiser.

During the forenoon the march to Petersburg began. The day was very warm, and the dust which rose as the column pressed on rendered the hot air stifling. The men suffered greatly from thirst. I do not remember any march more trying in this respect. Late in the afternoon we halted to rest. There was a strip of rough, broken ground on the right, a kind of ravine, about half a mile away. I went over there in search of water. Not a drop could be found. Returning to the column, I learned that there was water some distance to the left. Here was a beautiful spring of clear, cold water flowing in abundance. My intention was to drink very moderately; but I forgot all about this when I raised my quart cup, brimming full of the delicious beverage, to my lips. Of course I paid the penalty of my imprudence, and before dark was so ill that I was compelled to leave the ranks. I kept up with the column until after dark, but finally gave up all hopes of keeping with them, and camped till morning. The regiment, meantime, had reached the vicinity of Petersburg, and during the severe fighting there, had suffered some loss. Lieutenant-colonel Pattee was dangerously wounded. Lieutenant Steel, of Company A, received a terrible wound in the face. Abe Eshelman, formerly of the Eleventh, was mortally wounded, and died a few days later at City Point. The regiment was on a sandy ridge in front of woods, facing the rebel works, at a point nearly where the Norfolk Railroad passed through their lines. Behind them, in such a position as to fire almost over them, was a battery of rifled guns, which kept up a fire of shells upon the rebel works at intervals day and night. The rebel batteries responded at intervals of but a few minutes. This position was also under a continual fire from rebel sharpshooters, their balls reaching as far as the woods beyond with fatal effect.

The second day we were here, June 18th, William Rutter was mortally wounded. He had picked up a piece of corn-cake in the field back of the works. Some jesting remark was made about the cake and the rebel that made it, when he said he would go out and get some more. He was sitting in the pit beside me. He rose, still laughing, to carry out his purpose; but as his head and shoulders were exposed above the pit, there was a sharp "crash," and he grasped his left shoulder with his right hand and uttered a smothered exclamation of pain. A large rifle ball had penetrated and crushed the shoulder joint. He was taken back at once, and the arm amputated. It was reported that he did not survive the operation; but I have since learned that he lived till the 15th of July. We lost a number of men in this way and on the picket line.

The pickets were changed during the night, usually between nine and ten o'clock. This was the occasion for a lively time down on the line, in which the artillery usually joined. Sometimes this picket firing, with its accompaniment of booming cannon and screaming shells, would rise almost to the dignity of a night battle. In front, from the picket pits, rifles blazed and flashed with their crackling roar; and farther back, the great guns belched forth their lurid flames, casting a momentary glare over the weird scene. The gunners would range their guns before dark, so as to give the rebels a good one when the time should arrive. Every device was resorted to that would make this night-firing effective and annoying to the enemy.

Not long after the siege began, and while we were yet at this point of the line, we got a mortar-battery—two guns—into position. One clear, calm evening, the Yankees proceeded to try a little of this new-fangled music on our friends across the lines. The mortars were planted some distance to the right, and in such a position that we had a fine chance for observation. The line had been unusually quiet, as if the beauty of the tranquil sunset hour had subdued for a season the fierce spirit of war in the hearts of men. The sun's last ray had faded from hill-top and tree, and twilight was settling down upon the scene, when we heard on our right a strange, grumbling, muffled roar; and with a rushing sound, we saw what seemed two lighted tapers mounting upward, describing a curve through the air, and descending upon the rebel works, followed by two sharp, ringing explosions. There was a moment's pause, and then "boo-oom," and again two curves of light were marked along the dark sky, and the great shells descended upon the rebel works, exploding with a terrific crash. Still no reply from the rebel guns. Again the mortars boom out as before; but now, as if by a preconcerted signal, the batteries for about a mile along the rebel line cut loose at once, a perfect volley of cannon, all centered on the one point, around which the shells burst and flashed like a thousand thunderbolts. Not a cannon replied from our lines; only at intervals, for a while, would growl out that "boo-oom," and above the flash of bursting shells and flaming cannon would rise those two little points of light, curving slowly upward and then down, with a seeming deliberation that contrasted oddly with the whirl and bustle below. This continued a few minutes, and the "boo-oom" ceased. The little mortar-battery was "knocked out of time." Then there arose along our line a great "ha-ha"—an army laughing. Such was the spirit in which the men had watched this unequal combat. But the laugh quickly changed to a cheer, and a hundred cannon roared out their savage thunder from either line. Gradually the noise of strife died away, and an hour later the army slept.

As before noted, our rifle-pits extended along a sandy ridge, the ground open in front, sloping downward to the railroad. On our right the ground was somewhat rough and broken; but immediately in front, at the railroad, the ground rose abruptly for several feet, and then sloped gradually upward toward the rebel works. Toward the left of this point, the abrupt rise disappeared; but in general, the rebel works crowned elevated ground beyond, and the entrenched picket-lines of the two armies were in the open ground between the railroad and the rebel entrenchments. On the right, as you would go down from our trenches to the road, a kind of ravine extended toward the rebel works, and was commanded by their rifles. A large and well-manned picket-pit was established at its head, from which they sent their bullets hissing down almost without hindrance.

On the afternoon of June 19th, I think it was, word came in from our picket-line that ammunition was running short, and a fresh supply must be sent out. Myself and nine others were detailed to perform this rather delicate operation. The ammunition wagons were beyond the strip of woods in our rear, and we must run the gauntlet of sharpshooters, and risk odd shells in going and returning over this route, before getting started from the works. Taking each a piece of shelter-tent, in which to carry cartridges, we started for the wagons. If any man, that has been placed in similar circumstances, can say that he felt no unusual agitation, in view of the possible consequences, I must be allowed to suggest that he is got up on a different plan from myself. The truth is, I was considerably shaken up over the matter. It would seem quite heroic to be able to say that I was glad of it, when assigned to this dangerous duty. I am free to confess I was *not* glad of it. When selected for this purpose, I went through with it. The world looks very bright, on a fine June day, to a healthy boy of seventeen. He is not particularly anxious to exchange it for another, least of all by way of minie balls, when he has no chance to send back any in return. To do our work without faltering, it was necessary to count on a hurried burial down there between the lines that night. Whatever reckoning others made, this is how it seemed to me, and we might just as well look the probabilities square in the face.

Taking as much ammunition as each could conveniently carry, we returned to the rifle-pits, and thence to the skirmish-line. For some distance we had partial protection from the rifle balls, by crouching low as we walked; but as we advanced we drew the fire of the rebels more and more, as they discovered us and our object. At last we reached the ravine. It seemed as if a perfect stream of bullets was hissing down it; but we must pass. One after another we dashed through. As I passed, I turned my head to the right, and glanced up the ravine. The pit, at its head, seemed to smoke, from the rapid fire of its occupants. As I turned my head, a bullet clipped close to my face, and seemed to touch my hair. Onward we went, at the top of our speed, and soon reached the shelter of the high bank by the railroad.

Here we rested a few minutes. All were safe thus far. A fine spring bubbled out of the bank. How cool and refreshing its water seemed! Here were a number of men who had been shot on the picket line, some dead, others dying, one or two unharmed, caring for the wounded, until night should permit their removal. The sight of these mangled, bloody forms here was grimly suggestive. We must not *think* too much. The most dangerous part of our work still remained. The ammunition must go to the picket pits—must be carried there under the close range of rebel riflemen. During our progress thus far our pickets had kept up a sharp fire on the enemy. As we started for the pits the fight became more exciting. Both parties exposed themselves more recklessly, the rebels to shoot us before we could complete our mission, and our men to keep them down and make their fire less deadly. Bullets hissed at every step. I went toward the left, past several pits, I know not how far, and stopped at one in which was a lieutenant. Forgetting the situation for a moment, I stood upright, and stretched myself for relief from the weariness of carrying my heavy load. Instantly a bullet whizzed past my head, and dashed into a tree in the rear of the pit. Quick as a flash the lieutenant jerked me down, and warned me of the danger of exposure. After resting awhile, I started to return. Back to the railroad, again our only protection was the rapid fire and deadly aim of our riflemen. Thence to the main line, the only point we dreaded much was passing the ravine. The return was at last successfully accomplished. Notwithstanding the severity of the fire to which we were exposed but one of our number was injured—mortally wounded, I was told. Had it not been for the return fire of our own men not one of us would have reached the picket line alive.

This was my first and only visit to the picket line at this point. The same evening I was detailed for guard duty at brigade headquarters, where I remained till after July 4th.

On this part of the line it was not the custom to station videttes in front of the picket pits at night, as was usually done. A constant fire was kept up day and night. The boys used to invent various contrivances for the special benefit of the "graybacks." I have seen them work for hours to mold a bullet of such form as would make a particularly ugly sound, and then fire it across with a double charge of powder. But the favorite amusement was shooting iron ramrods. These could be picked up by hundreds over the battle-ground of the previous days, and, with a little careful fixing, could be made to fly with considerable accuracy. They were thought to have peculiar penetrating power, if they could be made to strike a picket pit with the sharp end. As they would send such an unusual missile whizzing through the air, they would laugh and chuckle over the anticipated consternation it would cause. One result often prophesied was that they would "string" a goodly number of the enemy on the ramrod. Whether such direful results were ever produced, we had no means of knowing.

Colonel Carle, of the One Hundred and Ninety-first, then in command of the brigade, had his headquarters in the woods about a hundred yards in the rear of the line. Here we were exposed to shells and stray rifle-balls, which occasionally reached us. The only damage inflicted was the loss of a quart of coffee, which was overturned by a fragment of shell striking in our fire while we were preparing dinner. About the same time one man was wounded at division headquarters, a few rods to our right.

It is remarkable how indifferent men become to danger under such circumstances. While myself and another soldier were engaged in washing some clothes one day, at a little stream to the right of this place, a bullet passed within a foot of our heads. The only effect was to turn our conversation to the subject of the range of rifles. It would naturally be supposed that, under such constant danger of death or wounds, men would be in continual dread of what *might* happen. As a rule, it is quite otherwise. Feelings of dread and uneasiness gradually give way to a sense of comparative security.

Coming under fire for the first time, a man usually feels as if he were about as large as a good-sized barn, and consequently very likely to take in all the balls, shells, grape, and canister, and such odds and ends, coming in his direction. After a while he begins to realize that he is not so large, after all, and frequent and continued experience confirms him in the view. That which unnerves the recruit is not alone the fear of injury or death to himself, but also the very nature of the terrible tragedy about to be enacted. He takes his place in line of battle as they are forming for a charge, knowing that hundreds of men who, now stand with him there in the full flush of life and health and the hopefulness of vigorous manhood, in one hour will lie dead in their blood, or be racked with the agony of shattered limbs or torn flesh. What man of ordinary humanity can be unmoved by such surroundings? No man should regard war otherwise than with the utmost horror, nor sanction it except as an awful, inevitable necessity. Some such feeling as this is in the breast of most men on the eve of battle, modified somewhat by the fact that the stern necessity is present. The difference between a recruit and a veteran is, mainly, that the latter has learned to command, perhaps to ignore, such feelings.

For my own part, I can remember few occasions when such thoughts did not oppress me during the waiting which is frequently incident to the opening of an engagement. These thoughts soon vanish amid the noise and excitement of battle.

You may ask whether soldiers feel any scruples as to shedding blood. I answer, first and in general, kill is the game. You know it, and prefer that the killing should be confined as much as possible to the parties over yonder. If this seems to you to be a cold-blooded way of looking at things, please remember I am not representing the ideal, but the real. Again, suppose the bullets are coming thick and fast from the woods over yonder, you soon discover that the only way to stop them is to send in your own as close as possible.

In firing, we always took aim, though often we could not see the enemy on account of trees or brush in which they were concealed. In such case we took aim at the point where they were supposed to be, guided by the smoke, a glimpse of a battle-flag, or the glitter of a gun here and there. The men were sometimes ordered to keep up a fire when not an enemy could be seen. The One Hundred and Ninetieth was generally sent on the skirmish line. The men always preferred this, and did not like it if this place was given to another regiment. Those who were not accustomed to skirmishing dreaded it. On the other hand, our boys were uneasy if placed in line of battle. As a matter of course, the skirmishers took aim in fighting. It was not seldom a question of marksmanship between two men, each the other's target. We took advantage of every thing possible in the way of "cover," the main point being to go ahead, stir up every thing in front, develop the enemy's position, drive in his skirmishers. A line of skirmishers is always thrown forward when the presence of an enemy is suspected. They will soon discover what is in front. Advancing at a distance of five paces apart, the loss is not so great as if a regular line were advanced in the same manner. In the Summer of 1864 the One Hundred and Ninetieth was armed with the Spencer rifle, an eight-shooter, and well adapted to work on the skirmish line.

Chapter IX.

JUNE 23d the brigade was withdrawn from this position for a day's rest. Our stay at this point had been almost equivalent to continuous fighting. We had lost men every day in killed and wounded. At headquarters we had received orders to prepare to move. After we were packed up ready to march, there was still a little delay before starting. Young Robbins and myself sat down with our backs against a tree, taking it easy. As we were sitting thus, a bullet came singing over, and struck the tree close to our heads. The ball was so far spent that it did not enter the tree, and was picked up by Robbins. We concluded this would do as a parting salute, and soon got out of that without any lingering regrets.

On the morning of the 24th the brigade moved to the left, and went into works before occupied by men of the Second Corps, on the Jerusalem plank-road. They should have reached this position before daylight, but did not. They could have reached the works with very little exposure by coming in a little further to the right. Instead of this, the column was led by Colonel Carle through open ground, less than eighteen hundred yards from rebel batteries. These, of course, opened on them with shell, causing considerable loss. Moreland, of our company, was among the killed. A shell struck him in the chest. The men, without waiting for orders, but without disorder, moved obliquely to the right, to reach the protection of lower ground, which there led up to the works. This called forth such violent protest and condemnation from Colonel Carle, that the result was a serious mutiny in the One Hundred and Ninetieth. Both officers and men felt that it was a blunder and an outrage to be thus needlessly exposed; and when Carle cursed them as cowards, they resented it. Confusion followed. The officers, almost to a man, refused to obey orders, or do any thing, until the insult should be retracted. The men were becoming dangerous. Carle rode up to Adjutant Wright, and ordered him to restore order, and take the men on to the works. Wright replied defiantly and profanely. Carle laid his hand on his pistol. Instantly a score of rifles were leveled on him. Yells and curses resounded on every side. He withdrew his hand, apologized to both officers and men, and they moved on to the rifle-pits without further trouble. Carle had the reputation of being a good officer; but it was said that he was under the influence of whisky at this time. I was with the brigade tent and baggage, and knew nothing of this until I visited the company the next evening. Neither do I remember who was in command of the regiment on this occasion. I think the colonel, lieutenant-colonel, and major were all absent, wounded. After we had been here a few days, arrangements were made to desist from picket firing; and after this we were no longer subjected to the peril resulting from this useless and barbarous practice. The loss of men from this cause was said to be about eighty a day in Grant's army, and was probably not less on the other side. Where the lines were so close, it was probably necessary and justifiable.

I remained at brigade headquarters until some time after July 4th, and was then relieved and returned to the regiment. It was then posted on the left of the Jerusalem road. Our camp was on sloping ground, the rifle pit at the foot of the slope. A few rods in front rose a slight ridge, and beyond this, a narrow fringe of timber shut out the rebel works from direct view. In this timber, or just beyond it, were our pickets. The well from which we obtained our supply of water was between our rifle-pits and the ridge spoken of. Further to the left, our line extended into woods, where the timber had been "slashed" in front for several hundred yards.

Back of where Company C's camp was, on the left side of the road as you faced the works, we soon after began the construction of a fort, called Fort Warren. It was four hundred feet square, strongly and carefully constructed. When finished, the ditch must have been twelve feet deep. The rebels did not get the range of our position at first, but annoyed us a good deal at times by pitching shells around at a venture. In a few days they would strike the vicinity of the fort with considerable accuracy, and kept at it with a persistence which showed that they were certain of the locality. After the work had progressed some time we felt no concern about the shelling. If it became too lively, we would stretch ourselves in the bottom of the ditch, and wait for the thing to let up, with great resignation, as we preferred this to working.

The confederate gunners had a way of sending shells "hopping" across, which was rather uncomfortable. One evening they were entertaining us in this fashion. The little ridge in front of our pits generally prevented shells from striking them, though the camp on the sloping ground behind was exposed. We had gone down to the works, waiting for the rebels to get through with their fun, which we regarded as comparatively harmless. We could see the flash of the gun, and by the time the shell would arrive, we would be safely sheltered behind the pit. One of these, however, struck the pit a few feet to my left. We waited a few seconds, expecting to hear it explode. Thinking the fuse had been extinguished, the men had risen up again and were indulging in jocular remarks over the matter, when, to our astonishment, the shell exploded in the air about ten feet high and nearly over the works, not far from where it struck. Where it had been during the intervening seconds we could not imagine. Fortunately no one was injured.

At this time, one of the men, who had not yet had supper, became impatient and started out for water. Just as he reached the well a shell came bounding over and struck him. A single exclamation of pain announced the result. Some of the men were at his side in a moment. A stretcher was procured, and he was carried back to the ambulance stand, to be taken to the hospital. The shell struck him about midway between the knee and ankle, leaving the fragment dangling by a few shreds.

While engaged in constructing Fort Warren we alternated in work with a regiment of colored troops. They were fine, soldierly fellows, and stood the shelling quite as well as any green troops.

At the entrance of the inclosure, of course, there was no ditch, a space being left about twelve feet wide. Passing along, one day, I saw a young colored soldier standing on this narrow passage between the ditches, curiously examining a twelve-pound shell which had been thrown over, and had failed to explode. Addressing him and taking the shell in my hands, I proceeded to give him a scientific explanation of how the thing worked. After expatiating at considerable length and in glowing language on the prodigious effects of such projectiles, I then unfolded to him the manner in which this particular sample might be exploded.

"Do you see that thing?" pointing to the fuse.

"Yes, sah, I sees him," replied the dusky warrior.

"Well, now, if I spit on that—the thing will go off. See here—*yeep! yeep!*" as I spat on it and hurled it into the ditch. With a yell and a screech a Comanche might have been proud of, that darkey "lit out." As he ran he turned his head, and seeing me dancing a war-dance to work off the extra hilarity which his fright had occasioned, he pulled up and joined in the laugh.

Work at this place continued about two weeks. One morning we were roused up before daylight and ordered to strike tents quietly. In ten minutes the column was moving down the plank road toward the rear. We went about half a mile and camped. The next morning we again struck tents before daylight, and moving toward the front, we formed line of battle in the rear of Fort Warren. Here we lay till after sunrise, when we returned to about the same place from which we had started. What all this meant was more than we could make out, but we supposed that an attack was anticipated.

We were then placed on picket still farther to the left. We called it picket duty; but as far as I could ascertain, we were the only force in front of the enemy on this part of the line. This ground had been fought over. The Second Corps had been driven from here June 23d, with heavy loss of men and guns. From the manner in which the trees were cut and splintered by bullets and cannon-shot, it would scarcely seem possible for a human being to remain alive on part of the ground. The loss had been terrible. Many of the dead had been buried in the trenches. Others, by the score, were buried where they fell, in rebel fashion, by throwing some dirt over them where they lay. Now, after the lapse of a couple of weeks, the dirt had washed from them, in some instances. Here and there you might see an arm, a leg, or a ghastly head protruding from a slight mound of earth. If any man was enamored of the glory of war, it was good for him to sit down and meditate in such a field as this.

Two of the boys sat down to their dinner, one day, near some bushes at the edge of the woods. The coffee was poured out, the frying-pan, with its contents of fried meat was beside the blackened coffee-cups. They were squatted on the ground on either side eating with a hearty relish, when one of them noticed more closely the bushes just overhanging the frying-pan, within a few inches of it. A human hand, dried, black, shriveled, protruded from the leaves, the distorted fingers in attitude as if about to make a grab at the contents of the pan. You suppose they turned away in horror at such an intrusion on their feast. Why so? The dead were all around us. When we slept at night behind the trenches, we made our beds by them. Under such circumstances human nature suffers a reaction, and horrors become the common things of life. These young men did nothing of the kind. With a light remark suggested by the idea of such a party wanting to rob them of their dinner, they moved the pan a little, and finished their meal. This done, they examined further, and found it to be the half-buried remains of a rebel soldier. On a scrap of paper they found the name, company, regiment, and State. The paper also contained a request for the burial of the body. They prepared a grave and buried him. Then as a matter of courtesy and humanity, one of them went out between the lines and was met there by a rebel soldier, to whom he related the circumstances, and requested him to join in this becoming duty by preparing a properly inscribed head-board. This was cheerfully done, and the board set up at the grave. In passing to and fro between the lines other dead were found, and these, too, were decently interred.

The days passed on pleasantly, and without special incident. No videttes were kept out, except in the night. None were needed, as the ground was open and level between us and the enemy. There was no picket firing, and we had a very comfortable time of it. We could watch the artillery "practice," which took place almost every evening, between the batteries on our right, without any apprehension that they would practice on us.

One evening I sat on the rifle-pit, watch-

ARTILLERY PRACTICE.   109

ing this. Scores of the men were doing the same, or were idling the time away as suited them best. The sun had sunk from sight; but as the shells would burst over the rebel redoubt, which was then the mark of our artillerists, they seemed balls of silver, in the rays of the sun, now invisible to us. Then they would expand, and roll away in little snowy cloudlets, almost before the sound of the explosion would reach us. Suddenly a great column of smoke shot upward from the redoubt; dark at first, but turning to a silver whiteness, as the rays of the sun touched it. A sound that seemed to shake the earth came rumbling through the air. A shell had reached and exploded the magazine. A laugh, with a cheer here and there, ran along our heavy picket-line. The rebels called out: "Stop laughing, Yanks!" "Stop that laughing!"

Whether this would have resulted in an outbreak between the pickets, is uncertain; but a moment later a shell came screaming across, about ten feet above the pits, passing a few rods to my right. Thinking this was but introductory, the men dived for the pits, and the laugh was suddenly and indefinitely postponed. Then a general "ha-ha" rose from the rebel pickets, and good nature was restored.

Some time in July I was taken sick with fever. I stayed a day or two at the surgeon's tent, but can not remember much about what occurred. I gave away every thing I had. Fortunately I gave my gun to Joe Bovard, who took care of it. I remember nothing of this, but he told me so afterward. I have also an indistinct recollection of being sent away in an ambulance, of being very sick at City Point, of the dull, dreamy indolence of convalescence. I was then sent to Davis' Island, New York. I improved rapidly during the voyage. I was here but a few days when I received a furlough, to report at Philadelphia, September 10th. The patriotic people of Pittsburg had ample and generous arrangements to care for the sick and wounded soldiers that passed through their city. Arriving there weak and dispirited, a gentleman met me at the train, and took me to a place where every convenience and comfort was provided. I had looked so long on the forbidding, bloody front of war, that it was a most pleasing revelation to discover that back here was the warm, loving heart of Peace.

Chapter X.

I ARRIVED at Philadelphia the night of September 10th. There had been a serious riot during the evening, between the soldiers from the hospital and some of those patriotic citizens who, although painfully loyal at times, have a great antipathy to blue. I reached the Citizens' Hospital without molestation. The next morning a large crowd of rioters gathered in the vicinity of the hospital, and a murderous raid was anticipated; but they dispersed without any demonstration.

From Philadelphia I was transferred, at my own request, to Little York, Pennsylvania. Although now quite recovered, I was detained here some time, in the hospital drum corps, as a musician. We went out one night, on the occasion of a Republican meeting. We started to parade the principal streets with a transparency, the usual following of small boys, etc. A crowd of patriots cheerfully greeted us with stones, brickbats, and like tokens of sympathy. We returned to headquarters in about twenty minutes, a demoralized outfit. The bass drum was broken, one drummer's head was peeled, the transparency was smashed, and we were mad. The managers gave us a dollar apiece; we disposed of our instruments, and started up street to look for any little incident that might afford balm for our wounded feelings. Opportunities were plenty, and many a cracked head bore testimony to the zeal with which the great national issues were discussed.

About the middle of October, myself and a large number of other convalescents started to rejoin our regiments, at the front. We went by rail to Baltimore, and remained over right at Fort Federal Hill, to go on by steamer, on the morrow. The "heavies," doing garrison duty here, were accustomed to dealing with recruits, and counted on making them step around in fine military style. This crowd was composed of men to whom soldiering was no novelty, and they had no fancy for extras. Hence, when they were ordered, with much pomp and assurance, to fall in line, in front of the barracks that evening, for roll call, at nine o'clock, there was something of a scene. The anathematical display has rarely been equaled in modern times. Perhaps twenty-five men out of several hundred at last took their place in a sort of line, with much gravity and feigned decorum, playing green, standing in any thing but soldierly attitude. Behind them, perched on the railing, windows, or wherever they could best see the show, was about as unruly and uproarious a crowd as could well be found. After vainly trying to bring order out of confusion, the sergeant, in great disgust, began to call the roll. A name is called:

"Here!"
"Here!"
"Here!"

On all sides the word "Here" is bellowed and screamed by a score of voices. The face of the burly sergeant grows red with fury, but he proceeds.

"John Smith."

Another chorus of hooting, jeering response, and then, in a momentary lull of the hubbub, a stentorian voice solemnly announces:

"He's gone to —— long ago."

This rather startling announcement is hailed with another outburst of laughter, yells, and cat-calls, interjected with allusions to the sergeant, which were far from complimentary. Finally, having exhausted his extensive vocabulary of maledictions on that mob of obdurate sinners, this patriotic officer took himself away, and the boys turned in for the night.

The next forenoon we went on board a steamer, but did not start down the bay till toward evening. The vessel may be called "steamer" as a matter of courtesy. The thing went by steam, but I would not care to ship a cargo of hogs on such a contrivance, unless they were of the kind that ran violently down the mountain. During the night the weather changed. A strong wind, with rain, swept across the bay. I was asleep on the deck when the storm came on, and awoke thoroughly wet and cold. Leaving my water-soaked blanket where it lay, I started to go below. The door was closed. A soldier, standing in the hatchway, suggested that by our united efforts we could push it open. I put my shoulder against the door, and he braced himself against me, and we gave a heave. The door went open and I went in, plunging headlong into the crowd lying on the floor, as close as packed herring.

Rascality.

Nobody swore, except those who were most severely bruised by our feet. There was an opening left in the side of the vessel, about two feet wide by twelve feet long. In the slow-going days before the war, this stately ship was probably used for transporting cattle, and the hole was made for the humane purpose of giving the animals air. Now it let in both air and water. I finally made my way down into the hold, and there, with the coal, dirt, and other things, found a more agreeable temperature. We reached Fortress Monroe the next evening. Here we were transferred to another vessel, and went up the James River, arriving at City Point the following evening.

This trip was very unpleasant. Besides the discomfort caused by the stormy weather, we were not provided with rations. No doubt provisions were furnished, and somebody got the benefit of them. On the second day those in charge of the vessel, in collusion with the officer in charge of our escort, proposed selling us lunch at the rate of fifty cents for a slice of meat and a piece of bread. Their enterprise did not pan out very well. But few bought, preferring hunger to submitting to the outrage. During the entire trip I ate not more than two ordinary hard-tacks.

Arriving at City Point, we were provided with a substantial supper. Our hotel accommodations, however, were not strictly first-class. Recruits and returning convalescents arriving here were provided with lodgings during their stay in a huge board structure known by the expressive name of "The Bull Pen." As to rooms, furnishings, and general appointments, the government had been exceedingly frugal. In fact, the entire outfit consisted of four walls, roof, and floor, joined together on principles of the strictest economy. The floor was comfortably carpeted with mud to the depth of about an inch and a half. Tobacco chewings, cigar stumps, etc., added variety and flavor.

On this particular occasion the institution was so crowded that you could not get room to lie down, all to yourself. This was no serious objection, as it furnished ample apology for resting your feet on the other fellow's stomach. Thieves found the "Bull Pen" an excellent place for plying their trade. The recruits and substitutes finding entertainment here usually had some money.

This night, after the lights were out, and all had been quiet for some time, I lay doubled up on the floor still wide awake. In such a gathering there are usually some splendid snorers. This crowd had some performers of rare merit. My location was toward the end of the building. Lying here, listening drowsily to the odd sounds about me, I heard a slight commotion down toward the center of the building, then a blow, and the cry of "Thief!" Then more blows, a general rising up of that part of the congregation, and a pouring out of profane objurgations that was surprising. The swearing and pounding went on with great vigor for some minutes, those not directly engaged cheering the others on with hoots and yells. In fact, a free fight was going on down there in the intense darkness, every body thumping every one within reach, thinking to spot the thief. Finally some one struck a match. As its flickering rays lighted up the gloom, they revealed a dozen or so of disgusted combatants glaring savagely on each other, and each wanting to know who was the thief. Of course it was impossible to find him now.

Chapter XI.

THE next day I reached the regiment, then on the Welden Railroad, near the Yellow Tavern. I say "the regiment." I mean what was left of it. Instead of the large, full organization I left in July, it was now but a remnant. Four commissioned officers of the One Hundred and Ninetieth remained. These were Colonel Pattee, Adjutant Wright, Captain Birkman, and Lieutenant Peacock. Of Company C, there were but ten men, myself making the eleventh.

A terrible calamity had befallen them at the time the Welden Railroad was taken from the enemy, August 18th and 19th. The brigade was sent forward to skirmish. They advanced and drove every thing before them till they struck the main force of the enemy. Here they fortified and held their ground without support until the afternoon of the 19th, when they were compelled to surrender. A few escaped by taking the suicidal risk of running through a gap in the rebel lines.

Mike Coleman, Captain Birkman, and a few others escaped in this way. Mike told me he heard men call "Halt! Halt!" on every side; but he looked neither to the right nor left, and went ahead. Dave Steen was killed in this battle. A ball struck him in the breast, a little to the right, and high up, severing one of the large blood vessels. As he fell, two of the men ran to him. He asked for his Bible—his only words. Hastily opening his knapsack, they handed it to him. Almost as his fingers closed on the holy book, his spirit hastened away from that scene of turmoil to the rest above. He was a brave soldier and a true man.

After the ground had been re-occupied, as it quickly was by men of the Ninth Corps, his remaining comrades buried him, and placed around his grave a rude framework to protect it from disturbance. The few that escaped, together with returning absentees, represented the organization under Colonel Pattee, who had now recovered from his wound. During September and October the regiment suffered considerable loss in fighting along the left of our line at various points.

On one occasion they were ordered to advance and "feel" the enemy. The design was merely to drive in his pickets, and compel him to show his strength. As soon as the command "forward" was given, away they went with a yell, sweeping the rebel pickets before them, and on into the works beyond, before the enemy knew what was the matter or could recover from his astonishment. An attempt was made to recall them as they went rushing on toward the rebel works; but signals and bugle-calls were unheeded. They entered, and for a time held a part of the rebel works. Of course, this could not last long. It was not the intention to bring on a general engagement, and they were not supported. In a little while they were driven back again with serious loss. Captain Kinsey, of Company C, was severely wounded, and never returned. In trying to bring Captain Kinsey off the field, young Overdoff was killed, shot through the head. When he first came to the company he was not very well liked; but his kind and pleasant bearing soon made friends of all. From his first experience in the Wilderness until his death, he was loved and honored as a brave and fearless soldier.

In the latter part of November the Ninth

Corps was passing, one day, and I went over to the road, and waited till the One Hundredth Pennsylvania came along. Here were many familiar faces. George Preston was there, his face as honest and bright as in boyhood's days; and George Dillinger—or was his name Hugh? Names become confused as the mind runs back over so many years. What I saw there was but a section of the past slipped forward, and given a different setting. My earliest recollections were connected with these faces, when, at church or school in the pleasant Summer-time, in one we listened to the good Irish pastor's "sixteenthly" and "seventeenthly" and "in conclusion" as sedately as our seniors; and in the other we took our regular flogging, as prescribed by the lamented Solomon. The stalwart boys in blue were the same boys still; but now they were the heroes of many a hard-fought battle. The hurried questions and answers of that brief interview touched upon as tragic scenes as ever employed the pen of genius. They told how one fell here, another there—dead for the land they loved.

December 7, 1864, we started on a raid, the object of which was to disturb the enemy's railroad communications toward the south. We followed the Jerusalem plank-road one day's march, reaching Notaway River in the evening, at Freeman's Ford. Our force was a strong one, consisting of the Fifth Corps, under General Warren, and a division of cavalry. With this force we felt quite at home within one day's march of the main army. Once across the river, and at a greater distance, we might stir up all the game we could take care of. Such was the feeling expressed by the soldiers as they discussed the situation on the march that day, and indulged in conjectures as to our probable destination and the outcome of the expedition. Of course, the company wag had a hearing while he expounded his views as to what we would do to the Confederacy or the Confederacy to us. The soldiers had confidence in General Warren, and regarded him as a prudent and efficient officer. He had the reputation of being personally brave and fearless.

As evening approached, we turned to the right from the plank-road, and halted in a corn-field, not far from the river. As we were about to break ranks we heard on our right the clatter and snapping of gun-caps, which, in a regiment armed with muzzle-loading guns, usually follows the command to prepare to load. This sounded like business; but nothing further indicating trouble occurred, and soon the cheerful camp-fires enlivened the scene, and we proceeded to make ourselves comfortable.

It was the general impression that we would soon move on, and make a night march; but as time passed, the men made down their beds, and addressed themselves to sleep. About ten or eleven o'clock, orders—perhaps delayed—were received for the men to camp for the night, the march to be resumed at two in the morning. It at once entered into the fertile brain of Lieutenant Peacock to extract a little fun from the circumstances. Going to a group of men sleeping soundly under their blankets, he deliberately roused them up and informed them that they could sleep till two o'clock.

"Well, what the —— did you wake us up for, to tell us that?"

"Why, you —— lunatic, are n't two sleeps better than one?"

Then would follow a volley of protestations and modified blessings from one side and the other.

At two in the morning we were again on the march. We passed Sussex Court House and a place called Corman's Well. In the evening we reached the North Cross House, on the Halifax road, thirty miles from Petersburg. Here we struck the Welden Railroad, and the work of destruction began. It was an exciting scene as the work progressed. There was an abundance of ties along the road, and of these fires were built beside the track. As far as the eye could reach the track was a line of blazing fires and busy, shouting men. A brigade would stack arms on the bank beside the track; then, taking hold of the rails, would begin to lift and surge on it altogether, shouting in unison:

"Ohé!"

"Ohé!"

"Set her *up!*"

"Ohé!"

Soon it would begin to give, and quickly would be hurled over from the road-bed with a ripping, crashing sound, followed by the shouts and cheers of the men. Then came the process of detaching the part thus overturned from that still undisturbed, if this had not been previously accomplished. Using a length of rail as a lever, this was quickly done, and in a surprisingly brief space of time the rails of a half-mile of road would be lying on blazing piles of ties. As a general rule, the rails were laid on the fire, and the heating of the middle portion would cause them to bend by their own weight, thus rendering them useless. When there was time, the men twisted the hot rails around trees or telegraph poles, or wreathed them together in fantastic shapes. We worked nearly all night. Toward morning we halted in a field, and slept for a couple of hours. Early in the morning the work was resumed, and continued till evening, with only brief intermission for dinner. It rained during the day, and became very cold toward evening. Night found us near a stream; I do not know whether it was the Meherrin River or a tributary of that stream. If the latter, it must have been near its junction with the river. The town of Bellefield is on the Meherrin. We tore up the road to that town. The town was held by a force of rebel infantry, and also artillery to the number of seven or eight guns.

A dismal storm of snow and sleet came on in the evening, and we could only anticipate a night of discomfort. Not long after dark we were ordered to fall in, with only arms and ammunition. The intention was to surprise the rebel force at Bellefield, or, at least, this was the belief of the men. If so, the project was abandoned. We crossed the stream, and tore up some more track, and returned. At this time the only man lost by the regiment during the raid was killed.

As we overturned a stretch of rail, as before described, he was caught under it as it fell. In the darkness and confusion no one noticed the accident but myself; and such was the noise and shouting, it was some time before I could make it known. As soon as possible we lifted the rails and drew him out. His chest was crushed by the great weight, and he scarcely breathed after he was extricated.

We spent the night standing around the fires. Sleep was impossible. The freezing mud was ankle deep, and, as the sleety storm swept by, it encased the outer world in an icy covering. Muffled in rubber blankets, crouched around the fires, to get what warmth and comfort they could, as the driving wind whirled the flames this way and that, the soldiers waited for the return of day.

The next morning the return march began. Flankers were kept out on each side of the column, to guard against surprise, and to prevent men from straggling out from the column, as it was known that rebel cavalry was hanging on our flank and rear, ready to inflict whatever damage they could. There was an occasional dash on our rear; but this was easily repulsed, and the day passed without special incident.

We camped that night in woods, two days' march from Petersburg. The storm still continued, but not so severe as during the previous night. I was fortunate enough to secure a piece of board, by means of which I provided myself comfortable lodging for the night. That board was torn from the side of a church near by. It was none the worse for that. Perhaps that church never before did any service in the cause of loyalty and the Union. That night it kept some Union soldiers off the wet ground. The next morning the march was resumed. Before we had gone far, we made a discovery that was enough to bring the blush of shame to the face of any civilized man. Some of our men, who had fallen behind in the march out, had been inhumanly butchered. I suppose the citizens, with their usual stupidity, thought we would never return, and no day of reckoning would come; and, finding these men in their power, murdered them with a cold-blooded brutality only equaled by the most degraded savages. Some were found riddled with bullets and stripped of their clothing; some had their throats cut, besides gunshot wounds. My first information was from Mike Coleman, who told me, with a look of horror in his face, of the blood-curdling sight he had just witnessed.

This discovery had a peculiar effect upon the soldiers. Even those who were usually undemonstrative gave vent to their feelings in hearty curses on the rebellion, and every thing connected with it. The wish was freely expressed that Lee might intercept us, and bring on the final battle between civilization and barbarism. Up to this time there had been no destruction of private property, except a mill, which had been burned as a war measure, and a house, from which a cavalryman had been treacherously shot; but now, either with or without orders, the men began to burn and destroy every thing within their reach. Even the fences were fired when it could be done. Not a single able-bodied man could be seen along the route; they had fled from the wrath to come.

The One Hundred and Nintieth was on the flank most of the day. About the middle of the afternoon, we reached a group of houses and outbuildings, which might almost be called a village. Here the head of the column halted, and the flankers drew in near the road. A large dwelling-house stood on the left of the road, the side on which we were. The buildings on the other side of the road were already in flames, and men were preparing to fire the dwelling-house. An old man was looking out of a little out-door kitchen. He was leaning on his staff, trembling with age, cold, and terror. A woman, bearing in her arms a babe but a few months old, came out of the house. Her pale face and quiet bearing, as she walked hurriedly away from the door, touched the gentler nature in the soldiers' hearts, that was now dominated by the tiger, which the sight of blood unjustly shed had aroused. Sympathy was marked on every face. Not an unkind word was spoken; but the house must burn. This general distress must teach the lesson that even *war* has its limit of barbarity.

That evening we recrossed the Notaway River, and camped about a quarter of a mile beyond, where we camped the first night out. Here we were joined by troops that had been sent down from Petersburg for that purpose.

A large house, perhaps a tavern, stood near the road, nearly opposite the site of our former camp. We had not been long in camp till we saw this house, and the buildings connected with it, wrapped in flames. From the fact that the place was not fired at once, we supposed it would be spared. The case was thus explained: When the men first came to the house, they were informed, on inquiry, that there was no man about. The woman who seemed to be the mistress of the house, claimed to be a widow. Investigation revealed a Springfield rifle and the uniform of a murdered soldier concealed about the premises. This was sufficient. The house was fired; and, as the flames spread, a man ran out from some place of concealment, and tried to escape. He received the mercy he had given.

During the night the sky cleared, and by

morning the ground was frozen. You would suppose that the soldiers suffered from the cold. Most of them slept as comfortably as you would at home, on such a night, covered over with your quilts and blankets. How was it done? Every man wore an overcoat, carried one wool blanket, a rubber blanket, and at least one piece of canvas tent, five feet square. We "bunked" at least two together, sometimes three. This gave two or three heavy wool blankets, as many rubber blankets, besides the shelter tents. If the ground was wet, we put a rubber blanket and a piece of tent under us; otherwise, only one of these, and the rest over us. Then, with a fire on one side, and a log on the other, there was no trouble about getting a good night's sleep. Such were our sleeping arrangements this cold night.

The march of the following day was very trying, because of the roughness of the ground and the extreme cold. In the evening we arrived in the vicinity of Petersburg, and took our place on the left of our lines, rather toward the rear. The loss of the Union forces during this raid was about one hundred, killed and wounded.

Chapter XII.

OUR camp was in woods. The ground was somewhat flat and wet, but with good facilities for draining. A deep ditch was dug around the camp on three sides. We had plenty of timber near the camp for building tents. The tents built by the soldiers for Winter-quarters were generally about nine feet by seven, built of logs, five feet high. A ridge pole was fastened up at the proper height, over which four shelter tents, buttoned together, were stretched and brought down to the top log on either side, and securely fastened. This formed the roof. The gable ends were closed with pieces of shelter-tent, boards, or some substitute.

A door about three feet high was left in the side next the company street. A chimney, with fire-place, was made at one end, carried up a foot above the roof. It was built of clay and sticks. Usually the tents were uniform in this respect, the chimney of each at the same side of the tent. Two beds or bunks, one above the other, were made of poles covered with a layer of leafy twigs, if possible. On these were laid wool blankets, rubber blankets, extra clothing, etc., making a very comfortable bed. Cracker boxes furnished material for door, seats, and table. The chinks between the logs were closed with clay mortar. The Winter-quarters of a regiment was simply a neat, cleanly village of small log houses, with this peculiarity, that only one row of houses faced on a street.

A military execution took place not long after our return from the Welden raid. A man had deserted to the enemy from a Maryland regiment, was captured, tried, and sentenced to be hung. The troops were ordered out to witness the execution. A hollow square was formed around the scaffold, and in due time the doomed man was led forth, accompanied by a guard, provost-marshal, and chaplain. The prisoner promptly ascended the scaffold, the sentence was read, and prayer was offered by the chaplain. The rope was placed about his neck, and an attempt was made to draw the cap over his head. It was found that the cap should have been put on first, and they loosed the rope to change it.

At this point the trap-door gave way, and precipitated them all to the ground. The straps with which the prisoner's knees had been bound were now loosed, so that he could again ascend the scaffold. He sat on the steps while repairs were made. When all was ready he took his place on the trap-door, first testing it with his weight, to see whether it might again give way prematurely. The cap was now drawn over his head, the noose adjusted, and the trap sprung. After he had hung for some time, we marched back to camp.

Our stay at this camp was very pleasant. The location was supposed to be unhealthy, and they issued whisky and quinine to the men for a while. This did more harm than good.

My tentmates were George Dunn, Joe Bovard, and Andy Shank. Joe Bovard had been in the service from the beginning of the war. He was over six feet in height, a good-natured, manly fellow. George Dunn extended upward to an altitude of at least six feet and a half, besides running along the ground an extraordinary distance before being started in a vertical direction. Our tent was larger than the ordinary, ten by twelve feet, well daubed and comfortable.

One day Jim M'Guire solicited "the hospitality of our tent for the purpose of entertaining some friends." This meant that they wanted to have a high old time, and our tent would be very convenient for that purpose because of its size. Early next morning the festivities began. Commissary whisky was provided in abundance. "Sport" (William Harris) furnished music for the occasion, which he extracted from an old fiddle procured from some unexplainable source. The ball opened with a good pull all around from the canteen. Ordinary forms of entertainment and social enjoyment soon became stale and they concluded to try the mazy dance. Our tent was floored with puncheons, and the racket which they kicked up was something marvelous. Occasionally I looked in to see how the thing was progressing. "Sport" was perched upon the upper bunk, his chin on the fiddle, his tongue protruding from his mouth, and wiggling to and fro in time to the the music, while on his face was a look of solemn intensity, as if his life depended on his efforts. The dances were necessarily limited to "French Fours," but these were rendered with great animation and in the latest style of art. As George Dunn would execute some of the fancy flourishes with which their figures were profusely ornamented, his head would bob against the canvas roof. This was suggestive. Procuring a stick of proper size, I crossed over to the rear street, and stood back of the tent watching my opportunity. Presently Dunn's head came bobbing against the canvas, and I brought the stick down on it with a good, sharp crack. The effect was all that could be desired. There came an unearthly bellow, accompanied, I grieve to say, with many exclamations suggestive of the future prospects of the culprit who had cracked the head of the festive dancer. Out they poured through the little door in hot haste to chastise the offender; but he was nowhere to be found. Failing in their search, they returned and resumed their exercises.

Although the day was quite mild and pleasant, there was some fire in the tent, and a thin column of smoke rose lazily from the chimney top. Thinking to add still further the spice of variety to the occasion, I took a cast-off garment and spread it over the top of the chimney, and awaited events.

Meantime within, the dance waxed warm again. The fiddle shrieked, the government stogies thundered upon the puncheon floor; but soon it was evident that all things were not as they had been from the beginning. Confusion first fell upon the fiddler. His dulcet notes, as they whirled through their lofty flight, reeled, and staggered, and fell, to give place to anathemas, steady and well sustained. Smoke filled the tent, and came creeping out through every crevice. They rose up as one man and cursed the chimney with great vehemence. They came scrambling out of the door, wiping their weeping eyes. A brief investigation revealed the cause of their discomfiture. In dislodging the offending garment from the chimney they nearly wrecked that ornamental structure. As soon as Shank saw what was the matter, he at once announced that "that —— had done it. He had played that trick on him once before, when he was getting dinner." From this and other remarks that were made, I thought it prudent to withhold all further co-operation. Toward evening the entertainment came to a close. This was hastened by unfavorable rumors from regimental headquarters. After carefully reconnoitering the position, I ventured to present myself at the tent. Dunn was deposited on the lower bunk, overcome by the varied duties of the day. The upper bunk had not proved equal to the emergency, and had broken down. The table, seats, and door were broken. The canvas roof was torn loose at one side and hung disconsolately from the ridge-pole. Shank was in the tent; Joe Bovard was sitting on a stump in front, evidently holding a discussion with his stomach. "Sport" was capering around with many sage remarks and comical gesticulations intended to express his sympathy. Just then Shank came out of the tent, and made for him, to chastise him for some offense. "Sport" fled up the street and across a little bridge to the parade-ground. The feet of his pursuer were heavy, and when he came to the bridge he paused, reflected a moment, and deliberately tore it up, and returned with a very satisfied expression of countenance, remarking:

"I've cu-cut off 'is communications off, anyhow."

This little episode of camp life seems to reach a very flat conclusion. But the facts leave no alternative. It required about two days' diligent labor to clean up and repair, to say nothing about Dunn's head, stomach, and general constitution. The working of prohibition was well illustrated in the army. If the traffic had been "regulated", as it is throughout a large portion of our country, the effectiveness of the army would have been destroyed within six months. As it was, the officers in charge of the commissary department were prohibited from selling to the privates. They tell us now that there is no use of trying to reduce drunkenness in this way. We cite the army as an illustration of successful prohibition. If men had been inclined to evade the law, they could have obtained liquor as readily as in civil life. If the evil had become manifest, a remedy could have been applied more directly than in civil life. But it was not necessary. If intoxicating liquors are made difficult to obtain, multitudes who would otherwise use them and become drunkards will not take the trouble to procure them. We affirm that this was demonstrated in the Army of the Potomac. There was very little drunkenness. A few would secure whisky, and become intoxicated. Sometimes it was accomplished by forging the name of an officer to an order. In the revel just described one of the men disguised himself in the uniform of an officer, and bought the whisky.

I never knew whisky to do the men any good. It was certainly one of the strangest of follies to issue whisky rations, as was sometimes done on occasions of peculiar exposure. The men who never tasted stimulants had the most endurance, and suffered the least from cold or exposure of any kind. We wonder at the delusions of witchcraft, and can scarcely comprehend how men could so abandon common sense as to give credence to such folly; but the absurdity of the use of alcoholic stimulants is not less puerile. The time will come when it will be told with pitying wonder how men of this day stupidly ignore the ghastly results of the liquor traffic to themselves and others, and with supine meanness bow their necks to the yoke which it fastens upon them. They will believe the most barefaced lies, assent to the shallowest sophisms of the liquor-dealers, and turn a deaf ear to the most evident dictates of common sense, justice, and prudence.

I think it is Thomas Carlyle says: "England has a population of thirty millions, mostly fools." The same comment is fairly applicable to every so-called civilized people in the world. The dealers say, "It is a benefit to trade." The fools echo, "We can not have prosperity in state, county, or town without the dram-shops." The brewers and distillers say, "It enhances the value of property and products of all kinds." The fools answer, with idiotic promptness and docility, "Yes, we must continue this ulcerous cancer upon the body politic—this unclean, pestilential, gangrenous sore, reeking with disease, vice, poverty, madness, to increase the price of grain." Yes, gentlemen, grain is more profitable deposited in the stomach of your son or your neighbor's son, in the form of whisky, mixed with sundry deadly drugs to give it "tone," than in pork, beef, or mutton, or transformed into the power which sets the whirling spindles of the East in motion, fires up the black caverns of a thousand furnaces, and fills unnumbered homes with joy and plenty. This would do very well if you saw fit to wait till the redeemed drunkard would recover health and manly ambition, and provide his family with sufficient food, clothing, and shelter. But there is a more direct way to turn your produce into money. Transform it into liquor. With this, arm the vampires that suck the people's blood, and turn them loose after him. Post them in every city, village, cross-roads. They will strip him, ruin him, finally kill him; but never mind that. They will make you quick returns in bright dollars. There is, however, one disadvantage incident to this method, which is worthy of consideration. The victims of the dram-seller die, and he must make more drunkards or his business will be gone. He may get his clutches on your boy. He will, if he can. This would be very unpleasant. However, if such a thing should occur, you can drive your son away, banish him from your sight. Then, if you should hear some time that he has ended the struggle with pistol, rope, or poison, thus decreasing the income of yourself and your partner, the dram-seller, you can console yourself with pious reflections on the mysterious ways of Providence.

Chapter XIII.

AT this time pickets were only changed every third day, "three-day picket," we called it. We preferred this, as it gave us such a long time without any duty of this kind, that the change was welcome. We were almost two months in this camp, and during this time I was only on picket twice. There was no enemy in our immediate front. The days passed as tranquilly and as free from danger as if war had never been. Now and then you could hear a boom of cannon far to the right; but if you wanted to see a rebel, you had to travel four or five miles to get a glimpse of one.

The second time I was on picket, the weather was extremely cold. The first day we were placed on reserve, at a substantial rifle pit, about fifty yards back of the regular picket line. During the night, for some reason, we had orders to strengthen the line. I was sent to the extreme right of our brigade line, where we joined with pickets of German troops. The posts were about a hundred yards apart, at each post a strong rifle-pit. The fires were built at the right or left of the rifle-pit, and carefully screened with bushes, so that those about them could not be seen from the outside. Our line here was in woods, and the timber was cut down between the posts. In front of the posts, videttes were placed during the night, who were relieved every two hours. The men at this post were from a Delaware regiment, and all strangers to me.

It was very cold work, standing vidette two hours at a time; in fact, my toes were slightly frosted the first night. We discussed the question, and concluded we could relieve matters a little. We arranged with the men on the post at our left to put out but one man from the two posts. By alternating, we would only be on post one-half as long. The officer in charge of the line would come from the left, and it was arranged that the other post would signal us when he approached, and one of us would go out. In this way we always had a man out from each post when he inquired into matters. This was rather an irresponsible way of running the Army of the

Potomac, but it seemed to us an improvement.

An incident occurred the second night, which convinced us that our plan was open to objection. The men were all sleeping around the fire, except one, a nervous fellow, of whose qualities I had not a high opinion. I must have been sleeping but lightly. Suddenly I was aroused by a noise outside the screen, to the right, as if some one had been passing stealthily along and tripped, falling headlong. I was instantly on my feet, and telling the men to scatter out and see what was the matter, I hastened out toward the right, followed only by the nervous man. We searched the ground carefully as far as the pit on our right. With our bayonets we thrust among the brush, and examined every dark corner, without any result. We returned, to find part of the men still at the fire, and the rest behind the rifle-pit outside. A similar search toward the left was equally fruitless. We never were able to explain the thing satisfactorily, but concluded to keep out our videttes.

After the Hatcher's Run campaign, I saw one of these men in rather unfavorable circumstances. We had been in camp a few days, and were engaged in building our tents, when we heard the sound of a fife and drum approaching. As they drew near, we saw a corporal and a file of men, and in their midst one of the heroes of the picket adventure, who had shivered over the fire that night, when he should have been out looking for the supposed intruder. Aross his back was hung a board, about three feet long by one in breadth, on which was inscribed, in large letters:

COWARD.

The musicians were playing "Rogues' March," to which the soldiers had adapted the following touching lines:

> "Poor old soldier,
> Poor old soldier,
> Bucked and gagged and sent to ——,
> Because he would n't soldier."

Chapter XIV.

THE morning of February 5th found our camp in a bustle of preparation. We had orders to march, leaving our tents "*in statu quo*," taking only overcoats, arms, and haversacks. General Warren was mounted on his old gray horse. This we regarded as a sure sign that a fight was on the programme. The column headed toward the left. Then we knew that Warren had done well to mount the old gray. A tender spot of the Confederacy lay in that direction. The "Southside Railroad" was the main artery that carried life-blood to the rebel army, and was guarded with jealous care.

The morning was bright, crisp, and frosty. The men were in excellent spirits. We had with us a number of waggish fellows that would be the life of any company, jovial, hearty, able to bring forth a joke under the most forbidding circumstances. One of these (Smith let us call him) had served eight years in the regular army before the rebellion, and had been in the volunteer service during the entire war. He was a sturdy, big-hearted fellow, now becoming somewhat gray with years. His favorite word was "Woo-haw," which he pressed into service quite frequently. From this we called him "Old Woohaw."

Some time in the forenoon we found the enemy intrenched at Rowanty Creek, just below the junction of Gravelly Run and Hatcher's Run. From a slight ridge about three hundred yards back, open ground sloped down to the run, where there were a few small trees on the bank, which sloped abruptly to the water. The stream was perhaps fifteen feet wide. On the other side the ground rose again as abruptly as on the side next to us; and on the bank were the rebel rifle-pits, this side of the stream being also covered with woods. It was not more than twenty-five or thirty yards from the side of the stream on which we were approaching to the pits beyond.

At this time I was armed with a Springfield rifle, muzzle-loader, while the rest had the Spencer. I never professed to have a natural appetite for cold lead, broken bones, etc., and very much disliked to go into a skirmish with a "long Tom." However, there was no help for it. The sharp crack of carbines showed that the cavalry had met with stubborn resistance. At the first halt after we heard firing, I loaded her up and was ready.

As the head of the regiment reached the ridge, we halted. The cavalry were keeping up a lively fire just ahead and on the right, and there was every prospect of an interesting time. Very soon we were ordered forward to skirmish. As the order was received, Smith remarked, with a peculiar twang to his heavy voice and an odd twist of his head:

"Now, boys, the woo-hawin' is a-goin' to begin."

We followed the road over the ridge, and filed to the right on a farm-road which led in this direction. As we filed right Colonel Pattee's voice rang out:

"Deploy, skirmishers!"

We came around the corner on a run, and as the order was given the men faced toward the enemy, and advanced as they deployed. Before the rear of the regiment had left the main road, the rest were charging down through the open field. They looked like a mob as they broke ranks and went pell-mell over the field, yelling like madmen. But there was method in their disorder, and before they had passed over half the distance they were in as good position as if they had gone about it in the most formal manner. It was a reckless movement; but the officers were not responsible for it, as no order was given except to deploy.

Reaching the stream, we found it covered with ice, on which we hoped to cross. One of the foremost boys stepped upon it, and it at once gave way, and let him into the water. Just the top of his head stuck out above the fragments of ice. He was fished out as expeditiously as possible, and the idea of crossing in that way was abandoned. Men came down with axes, and proceeded to fell trees across the run on which to cross. While this was going on, we did our best to keep the rebels down behind their works, and render their fire ineffectual. We soon succeeded in this, but not until they had inflicted some loss. Sullivan was standing a little below me, when a bullet clipped by his left hip, cutting his pants about three inches, but doing no harm. A ball touched my hand as I was capping my gun. Others struck close around. Soon the trees were down, and part of the men crossed, while others kept careful watch on the rebels, and fired rapidly to keep them down. When enough had crossed, perhaps forty or fifty, then every body yelled, and those who had crossed charged the pits, and the rest came crowding over. Some of the rebels surrendered, and a few escaped. As the final charge was made, the line of battle came down, reaching the run just in time to lose some men. There may have been some reason unknown to us for bringing them down; but as far as we could see, it was a mistake. Our loss was fifteen wounded and one or two killed.

The losses of a regiment do not always show its courage nor its effectiveness as a military organization, but rather its lack of discipline, and unskillful handling. The One Hundred and Ninetieth was composed of well-trained, veteran soldiers, and had good officers. This fight shows how such a regiment may incur serious disaster without room for just reflection on the skill, courage, or discipline of men or officers. Had a much stronger force been behind those works, situated as they were, our heedless charge would have resulted in a bloody repulse, unless speedily supported by a charge from the line of battle, which would have involved heavy loss.

The road which we had followed is called the stage-road. Crossing the run, we followed it in the direction of Dinwiddie Court House, until we reached the Quaker road. The enemy was not encountered in our front, but farther to the right there was severe fighting along Hatcher's Run. During the night we moved to a position near Dabney's Mill. I think we followed the Vaughan road. In crossing Gravelly Run, there was some delay in getting the column over. After we had reached the other side, and were waiting for the others, a colonel offended one of the men of Company A, ordering him away from a fire by which the colonel was standing. This called forth some of the liveliest sort of vituperation. Such combinations of opprobrious epithets are rarely exhibited. That man's relatives, near and remote, male and female, were brought into requisition to define the exquisite meanness of his nature and origin. The discomfited nabob appealed to Colonel Pattee for redress, who sent Adjutant Wright back to quiet the boys.

During the day we moved out from our position near the run, into the woods in front, and formed line of battle. The One Hundred and Ninetieth was in the line. The day was dismal. Rain and snow had fallen during the preceding night, and now it was growing colder. Our line advanced over ground partly swampy. In maneuvering to pass one of these difficult places, the Two Hundred and Tenth Pennsylvania was massed behind us, and came crowding close after. Some of the men would break through the crust of ice, and sink into the mud beneath. Among others, George Dunn, notwithstanding the size of his feet, went plunging in, half-way to his knee. When the foot was withdrawn, it was found that the shoe had been left in the depths below. George hesitated, thinking, perhaps, to attempt a rescue; but it was too late. The Two Hundred and Tenth, coming on in close divisions, trampled it down beyond all hope of recovery. Advancing some distance, the line halted. The formation of the Second Division must have been imperfect, on account of the nature of the ground. This probably caused the delay.

On the right a severe engagement was in

progress, and in front was some skirmishing. The men, as usual with them when placed in line of battle, were uneasy and dissatisfied. Soon they began to go out, one at a time, then by twos and threes, toward the front. No objection was made by the officers, until the line began to grow thin. A little later, part of the line became engaged; but, as the right of the corps had been checked, we were soon withdrawn, and took a position not far from the run, where we intrenched and held the ground. Here we were on the left, where our line rested on the run. We were considerably annoyed by shells, which came nearly from our rear. Our pits faced down the run, and afforded no protection from shells coming from the enemy's position at our right.

On the morning of the 8th we had orders to "fall in," and soon we were in line, ready to move. Passing to the right a short distance, we halted, at a gap in the rifle-pits, where a road led out to the front; I think it was the Vaughan Road. Soon an aid rode up to Colonel Pattee with orders. Some one inquired, of those standing nearest the colonel, what the orders were. One of them replied, with the utmost seriousness:

"The orders are for the One Hundred and Ninetieth to report in —— in less than ten minutes."

We passed out on this road some distance, and then bore to the right, over ground strewn with dead horses, that had been killed during the cavalry fighting of the preceding days. After advancing about a mile, we halted in open ground, and formed line of battle. On our right, and some distance in front, was timber. We hastily intrenched, for this purpose tearing down a house. We judged that the enemy would not let us remain long undisturbed; nor were we mistaken. Through the still, frosty air we heard the sound of preparation. We could hear the officers giving orders, and the snapping of caps as they prepared to load. Their line of battle extended far past our left, and a line was evidently preparing to come down on our right flank. We threw up pits on each flank, and waited, uncertain of the result. We knew of no arrangement to prevent our being overwhelmed by numbers. This suspense continued for some time, and we expected every moment that the vengeful storm would burst upon us. But now an aid was seen galloping toward us, and we were ordered to withdraw from our exposed position. We lost no time in regaining the works we had left in the morning. What this little side show was for, we could not imagine. Perhaps it was a misunderstanding.

The same day we recrossed Hatcher's Run, and began the construction of permanent works on that side. We worked by reliefs, three hours on duty and three off. We had run out of provisions, and a fresh supply failed to arrive. The men became dissatisfied, and finally refused to work. Threats of compelling them to work were made. The men answered by gathering up their guns and starting for the woods, in the rear. At this point General Warren came down and spoke to the men in a reasonable manner. The mere fact of his coming among them had a good effect on the men. He urged the necessity of the work, and told them that if provisions were not on hand by a given time, he would consent to their ceasing from work. The men then went to work cheerfully.

Jack M'Bride and myself had previously solved, in a measure, the difficult problem of reconciling the conflicting claims of an empty stomach and the vigorous prosecution of the war. As night came on, we retired some distance into the woods, built a fire, and made ourselves comfortable. The next morning we found a piece of pork, which had been lost or thrown away three or four days before. It was good. We scraped the mud from it carefully, and ate it with a relish. We then came back and went to work with the rest.

After these works had been completed, we moved some distance down Hatcher's Run, to a small branch of that stream, called Arthur's Creek. Our position was on the left flank of the army, facing rather toward the rear. For the third time this winter we built winter-quarters. Our camp was pleasantly located, fronting a large farm, in the rear woods. Brigade and division headquarters were in the woods, our picket-line in the open ground beyond the farm-house, a mile from camp.

On the 7th of February, the next day after the fight near Dabney's Mill, I got a Spencer rifle, and kept it until we were mustered out. The spiral spring of the magazine was damaged in some way, so that it would receive only four or five cartridges, instead of seven. I repaired it by taking the spring out entirely.

It would then receive nine or ten, and a little practice made the experiment a success.

Duty was light, and our main business was amusing ourselves. For in-door amusement, euchre was the favorite. There was not much gambling, but many fine points were settled by "best three out of five." One form of out-door amusement was the following: A peg was driven into the ground, and to this were fastened two ropes, fifteen or twenty feet long. Two men were then blindfolded, and placed one at the end of each rope, on opposite sides of the peg. To one was given a notched stick, about two feet long; and also another, to rub over it, making a scraping sound. He was called the "scraper." To the other was given a pant-leg, or something of this kind, stuffed with paper or rags. He was called the "pounder," and it was his business to "pound" the scraper, if he could. They were each required to keep hold of his rope. The boys would sometimes stand around a circle of this kind by the hour, and watch the fun. The two would move about with cat like caution, each listening for the other. Sometimes the pounder would think he had the other, *sure;* and, listening most earnestly, anticipated triumph shining from his face, he would bring his weapon down on nothing. Again, the scraper, thinking the pounder, who was right beside him, was far away, would rest the end of his notched stick on the ground, and draw the other along it, "scrape-scrape," when down would come the pant-leg on his head, followed by shouts of laughter from the audience.

The soldiers built a large tent for religious meetings, and a revival of extraordinary interest took place during our stay here. The noble Christian young men who did this work remember those meetings with satisfaction now, whether they are on earth or in heaven. They conducted them without the aid of a minister. No! they themselves were ministers of God, anointed from on high for this work.

Some of the conversions were remarkable. One young man, whom I had known as a brave, fearless fellow, was converted during a meeting of peculiar power. The change was plain and evident to all. His handsome face was continually bright with the peace of God. He fell in battle, March 31st, and died in the arms of his comrades, who were trying to carry him back when our line was broken and routed.

As Spring drew near came the reviews and various movements that indicate the approach of active operations. Some changes were made in the brigade. It now consisted of the fragments of three Pennsylvania regiments, the One Hundred and Ninetieth, One Hundred and Ninety-first, and One Hundred and Fifty-seventh; two Delaware regiments, now consolidated into one, and the Two Hundred and Tenth Pennsylvania. The latter was a one-year regiment, and almost as large as the rest of the brigade. They were a fine body of men, reliable and well-drilled. There were but five commissioned officers in the One Hundred and Ninetieth. Colonel Pattee and Adjutant Wright, Captain Birkman, Lieutenants Coleman and Peacock. Captain Birkman had charge of Companies A, B, and C. The One Hundred and Ninetieth and One Hundred and Ninety-first acted together as one regiment, under command of Colonel Pattee. The fragment of the One Hundred and Fifty-seventh—not more than forty or fifty men—was regarded as a part of the One Hundred and Ninety-first.

We held this little band in high esteem. They were heroes, every man of them. Captain Carter was in command. We were the Third Brigade, Second Division, Fifth Corps.

Chapter XV.

THE BEGINNING OF THE END.

ON the morning of March 25th, I know not why, our camp was astir earlier than usual. Heavy cannonading could be heard toward the right, but this was nothing uncommon. As time passed on, the noise of strife continued, and seemed to extend farther toward the left. Eating a hasty breakfast, I started toward the scene of action, determined to ascertain the cause of the unusual uproar. When starting from camp, I did not suppose it was any thing more serious than an artillery fight of more than ordinary interest. As I went on the sound swelled to a steady roar, which showed that a determined battle was in progress. Drawing nearer, I saw the troops in line of battle, the shells bursting, and cannon flaming as far as the eye could reach.

I was informed that Fort Steadman had been taken, and a part of our works captured by the enemy. Supposing that we would be ordered to the right to retrieve the disaster, I started to return to camp. I had not proceeded far when I saw the head of the column approaching. I hurried back to camp and procured my gun and accouterments and started to overtake the troops. I was joined by Lewis, who had also been absent. Only the pickets and ordinary camp guard remained. As we passed along we met President Lincoln, General Meade, and staff, coming toward the left. We concluded to greet them with due ceremony. As we met them we halted on the bank by the road and presented arms. The President raised his hat, and turned to General Meade with some humorous remark as they rode on. It seemed a reversal of things for the head of the nation to pass in review before a couple of stragglers.

We found the Second and Third Divisions drawn up in the rear of the works as support, awaiting events. A large number of prisoners passed to the rear while we waited here. Farther to the left, the First Division advanced on the enemy's works, and was repulsed with considerable loss, but succeeded in establishing our lines nearer to those of the enemy. We were not engaged, and returned to our quarters in the evening.

The next morning I started early to visit an acquaintance belonging to the One Hundred and Fifty-fifth Pennsylvania, First Division. It was not yet sunrise when I reached their camp. The acquaintance whom I had come to visit was on picket, and I went out along the line to find him. The pickets were stationed in woods, and the men were engaged in building or strengthening their intrenchments. Passing along the line, I noticed that the men kept close to the pits. I inquired if things were woolly out there, and was informed that the latitude was decidedly unhealthy.

I now noticed a Yankee vidette about twenty-five yards in front, rifle in hand, sticking close to a tree, and scarcely fifty yards farther on, a rebel vidette peered cautiously past another tree. The vigilance with which they watched each other revealed both the danger and security of the situation. If all were watching each other as jealously as these, I could continue my observations with comparative safety. A little farther toward the left I reached open ground. Arrangements had been made, under flag of truce, for burying our dead who had fallen in the battle of the previous day. Quite a number of dead lay scattered over the field, some of them close up to the rebel works. They were carried back within our own lines and buried there. They were carried on blankets, one man taking hold of each corner, and thus bearing them along.

Four men thus engaged, halted with their burden to rest as they were passing near me. In the blanket lay a boy, certainly not more than eighteen or nineteen years old. At first glance you could scarcely believe that he was dead. Surely the grim King could not stamp upon dying clay a smile so pleasant, a laugh so winning, as shone out from those parted lips and half-closed eyes! But just over his heart, half-concealed by his arm, that bloody rent in his blouse showed how he died.

"Somebody's darling is cold and dead."

I looked upon that handsome, boyish face with wonder. The smile was so happy and so life-like that the first impression was only that of light and careless mirth; but the lines curved away into an expression of solemn majesty, is if the passing spirit, thrilled with the full perception of the grandeur of its own immortality, had left this impress on the tenement of clay.

On the way back to camp, evidences were everywhere visible that the final act of the great national tragedy would quickly come on. That afternoon I made ready for active operations by purchasing from the "commissary" a couple of pounds of extra coffee. The regulation quantity was sufficient while in camp; but after a hard day's march there was a strong inclination to throw an extra handful into the old coffee-pot. As a result, the inexperienced frequently found themselves short after a few days, to their discomfort and actual disadvantage.

Chapter XVI.

THE next morning, March 27th, I went on picket. Some time after midnight, on the 28th, we were withdrawn, and returned to camp. Orders had come to prepare for the march. The camp was astir with busy life. In a little while our tents, that looked so neat and trim last evening, with their white canvas roofs and clean-swept streets, will be silent, cheerless, and deserted. My tent-mates had taken down our shelter-tents, and I had nothing to do but pack my knapsack, and all was ready.

In some of the dismantled tents the fires still burned, casting their flickering rays upward through the air, while about them, sitting or lounging at ease, were men equipped for the stern work of war, ready to fall into line at the word of command. The stirring scene had in it not a little of sadness. We had passed pleasant hours in this camp. That tender something of association which clings around the thought of "the old campground" breathed through the darkness that night, and glanced in the camp-fires that dimly lighted up the warlike scene. These would be our last Winter-quarters. For some, the next night would bring the quiet "bivouac of the dead."

The strength of the Fifth Corps was as follows:

    First Division, General Griffin, ... 6,180
    Second Division, General Ayer, . . 3,980
    Third Division, General Crawford, . . 5,250
            Total, ... 15,410

The artillery consisted of twenty guns, and there was an escort of forty cavalry.

The march began at three o'clock on the morning of the 29th, the Second Division in the advance. We passed down what was called the stage-road toward Rowanty Creek, the same road on which we had marched February 5th, at the time of the Hatcher's Run fighting. We reached the vicinity of the creek a little after daybreak, and formed line of battle in the open ground south-east of the residence of W. Perkins. Much to our dissatisfaction the One Hundred and Ninetieth was placed in the line, and the Two Hundred and Tenth was deployed as skirmishers. They did not advance till the line was formed, and then not far enough ahead of us to be of any use. Fortunately no enemy was found; but time might have been saved by a prompt advance of the skirmishers without waiting for the line.

Crossing Rowanty without opposition, we followed the stage-road to its junction with the Quaker road. Up this we marched toward Gravelly Run. The First Division, however, followed the stage-road some distance farther. How far we advanced up the Quaker road I am unable to say; but we finally turned to the left, and formed line of battle, facing the west. In our front was quite an expanse of open ground sloping down toward woods beyond. About a hundred yards to our left was a battery, ready for action. The Two Hundred and Tenth was again sent forward to skirmish. They advanced with due form and ceremony until they neared the woods, when they opened fire with such a racket that we supposed the enemy had been found in force. But they soon let up, and presently sent back a solitary prisoner, about as forlorn, dilapidated looking a specimen of grayback as could be imagined.

While we were waiting, John Edgar went down to the battery, in which he had served for a considerable time, detached from his company for this purpose; but he had left it and rejoined his company without being returned in due form. He was at once placed under arrest as a deserter by the officer in command, the man whose brutal treatment had caused Edgar's unauthorized return to the regiment. This made quite a commotion, and might have produced serious trouble; but as soon as Colonel Pattee learned what had occurred, he went down to the battery, and demanded and secured Edgar's release without delay.

After remaining here some time, we moved farther toward the left. Here the One Hundred and Ninetieth deployed as skirmishers, and advanced into the woods, facing the south-west. We remained in this position during the night. Meantime the First Division had passed up the Quaker road. At an old sawmill about half a mile from the Boydton plank-road they encountered the enemy at four in the evening. A brief but terrific conflict ensued, in which the enemy was driven back to the junction of the two roads. We knew from the rapid discharges of artillery and the heavy volleys of musketry that the great struggle had begun. The First Division lost 367 killed and wounded, while the loss of the enemy was heavier.

At dark on the 29th rain began to fall, and continued during the night and the following day, making the roads almost impassable. On the morning of the 30th we left the position held during the previous night, and moved up the Quaker road. Near the sawmill we turned to the left, and crossed the Boydton plank-road near Mrs. Butler's. In the field there were dark patches of blood on the ground, here and there, which the rain had not yet washed out. Guns that had dropped from the hands of wounded or slain, knapsacks, haversacks, accouterments stripped from mangled men ere they were borne from the field, lay scattered on the ground over which we passed.

Near the plank-road, we deployed, and advanced across a branch of Gravelly Run. The right of the regiment rested in open ground, near a negro's house, and the left extended into the woods in a north-west direction. I think the division formed on our left, facing the Whiteoak Road; and we held a gap in our lines, between the Second Corps and our own. Companies A, B, and C were on the right, in the open ground.

In advancing to this point, we were under a sharp fire, to which we did not respond, but hastened to throw up pits. On the left of the regiment the firing was lively, as the men in the woods did not need to be in such haste entrenching. We were ordered to "rally by fours," and each group threw up a separate pit.

I was in the group with Mike Coleman, and had a chance to notice one of his peculiarities. As we advanced to this position, he seemed to be dazed, and almost unconscious of his surroundings. When we halted to entrench, with my most vigorous exhortations I could not arouse him to any interest or exertion. We had no shovel, and must make a pit with rails and stones, which we could gather up in front. I would urge him to carry stones and put them in place. He would perhaps pick up a couple, very leisurely, and lay them on the ground, back of the pit, and then stand with his hands in his pockets. The bullets would whistle around, or strike the ground near him, and he would look about as if he did not understand what it all meant.

Yet in battle, he was always cool, brave, and daring.

In a little while we had a pit, capable of stopping a rifle ball, and considered ourselves ready for any ordinary emergency. During the day, the rebels attacked the line on our right, and were repulsed, after a sharp fight, with considerable loss. They also advanced in our front, and opened fire on us; but only as accessory to the more determined movement on our right. The left of the regiment returned the fire; but we could not see the enemy, and there seemed no reason to justify a random fire.

There was a man in Company C who was usually troubled with a deficiency in his knees at such times. Though sufficiently warlike and lion-hearted by nature, no doubt, yet his legs were his undoing. They worked very well, when steered for the rear, but otherwise they were a failure. When the firing began on the right, he took his position behind the pit with an air of great determination. Pointing his gun—a Springfield rifle—toward the enemy, he sat crouching low, and looking intently toward the brush in front. The boys were sitting or standing around, dividing their attention between the skirmish, partly visible through the trees, and R——, whose warlike attitude and evident terror called forth good-natured raillery.

"Steady on the left, R——!"
"Cut her loose, R——!"
"Give 'em ——, R——!"

Such were a few of the cheering exhortations which greeted that redoutable warrior. To all these he paid no heed. I suppose, in spite of his fears, a few shells, a sharp volley, or even a charge from the enemy, would have given him profound satisfaction—if unharmed himself—as a vindication of his prudent vigilance. Nothing of the kind occurred, and soon things resumed their former comparative quiet.

There was not much done during the day, except to get troops in position and prepare for the struggle of the morrow. There was some skirmishing, but our losses were not heavy—less than two hundred in the two corps, the Fifth and Second.

As night approached, a vidette was placed in front of each pit, near the edge of the woods, which was about forty yards in advance. It was not yet dark when the first man was posted here, and fire was at once opened on him, by invisible marksmen in the woods.

At first the bullets went whistling over, but soon they came lower, and began to strike the fence by which he was standing,—right, left, close,—with a savage snap. Up to this time our vidette stood it with seeming indifference; but, as the splinters began to fly from the fence, his indifference gave place to a lively interest, which called forth the laughter of the sympathizing spectators. He threw down his gun, and hastily piled rails together for a protection, and took refuge behind them.

Night came on, dark and gloomy, the rain continued to fall, and the soldiers lay down on the water-soaked earth to take what rest they could. I made a comfortable bed, by leaning two rails against the rifle-pit. On these I bestowed myself, and drew over me my rubber blanket. My knapsack was placed under my bed, to protect it from the rain. My haversack served for a pillow, and, with my cartridge box, which had not been removed since the morning of the 27th, still strapped around me, and my rifle in my hands,

I sank to sleep, the rain pattering on the blanket over my head.

About four o'clock, Sergeant Hasler woke me up to go on vidette post. I arose and followed him in the deep darkness. Reaching the man whom I was to relieve, instructions were given in a whisper, and in a moment I was alone.

This was the last watch of the night, and if a surprise was contemplated by the enemy, the attempt would be made during these two hours. The rebel pickets were close at hand, and occasional sounds and voices had been heard by my predecessor. The rain dripped monotonously from the trees, and now and then a breath of wind moaned drearily through their branches. The ear alone could detect approaching danger; and thus, with rifle in hand, I listened, jealously noting every sound.

Time passed on, and at length the almost painful darkness began to disperse. Objects very near could be indistinctly discerned. What if all those weary men back there should sleep till clearer light should made me a mark for the unseen foe, that did such good shooting last evening? Why were not the videttes, at least, advanced into the underbrush, instead of being posted at its edge, to be shot at by rebel sharpshooters? Thoughts like these were running through my mind as daylight approached. But all anxiety was allayed before long, by the sergeant calling me to come in.

Chapter XVII.

WE made a hasty breakfast, and then the waiting of the preceding day continued. Every rifle stood loaded where it could be grasped in a moment. As time passed on, there was an evident uneasiness on the left. About ten o'clock, the occasional picket firing increased to the sharper rattle of skirmishing, and then deepened to the roar of battle, as the sound of continuous volleys rolled through the woods, mingled with the bellow of cannon and the hiss of shells. Every man now stood with rifle in hand, ready for the decisive moment which had evidently come. Above the noise of musketry and cannon we could sometimes hear the well-known rebel yell, and knew that they were charging with all their force. Now the horrid uproar could be heard moving backward toward the run. But now orders have come. Word is immediately sent along the line to assemble on the right. The Sixteenth

Maine will relieve us. Colonel Pattee mounts his horse.

"Fall in!"

"Right face!"

"Forward, double quick, march!"

We plunge into the woods, following the road toward the left. Shells crash through the trees, and bullets patter around like hail. The left of the division was flanked and hopelessly turned. The right was stubbornly resisting, but giving way before the overpowering force that was crowding down upon it. We halted and faced the front, advancing a short distance from the road toward the fighting. Wounded men were limping past. We could see the smoke through the trees, and the men slowly yielding, fighting as they came.

Colonel Pattee gave an order, but we could not hear a word. We all knew what it ought to be, and instantly deployed. The line, broken and shattered, went back past us, and we met the enemy with the rapid fire of our repeating rifles. We brought them to a stand in our front. If fresh troops could have been thrown in on our left, the disaster could have been retrieved at this point, and the rebel charge hurled back; but our flanks were exposed, and we were many times outnumbered, and in danger of being surrounded. There was nothing left but to get out of that the best we could.

Colonel Pattee rode to and fro along the line, mounted on his bay horse, encouraging and directing his men, steadying and inspiring them by word and example. Under a less devoted commander we would have been captured or driven ingloriously from the field. Before we reached the edge of the woods, the enemy had inclosed us in the form of a V, and were pouring their fire upon us from the front and both flanks. We brought out most of our wounded, but some had to be abandoned. Except these, not a man was taken prisoner. Reaching the edge of the woods, I knew that no stand could be made before crossing the branch of Gravelly Run. I "stood not upon the order of my going," but went at once, and at a lively pace. Colonel Pattee was the last man to leave the woods. He came down across the narrow field, crouching close to the neck of his horse, which was reeling and staggering from wounds out of which his life-blood gushed at every plunge. Leaping from the back of his dying steed, he rallied his men on foot.

The trees on the side of the ridge which sloped down to the stream opposite the open ground in which we had intrenched on the 30th, afforded excellent cover. Here most of the One Hundred and Ninetieth, and some from other regiments, rallied and faced the enemy. We were not much more than a heavy skirmish line; but the tide must be stayed here, at any cost. The rebel lines came surging on, elated with victory; but before our steady fire they wavered and came to a halt. Thus, with scarcely the space of a hundred yards between us, we stood and poured at each other showers of deadly missiles. Rebel shells from somewhere on our right were grinding through the trees and bursting all around, while the fire from their infantry was beating on our thin line with terrible effect. A man close beside me was struck through the face with a rifle ball, and walked back toward the rear, pale and bleeding. Casting my eyes toward the left, I saw our color-bearer holding the flag, his face deadly pale. Brave old Woo-haw had just been struck down by his side and carried to the rear. Mike Coleman was in his glory. Miller's face wore its accustomed smile as with grave deliberation he loaded and fired.

But this state of things could not long continue, and the most hopeful were growing anxious. A few hundred were fighting the force that had driven a division. But just now on the ridge behind us, a battery wheeled into position, and sent charge after charge of grape and canister whizzing across into the enemy's ranks. Still they did not give way, and the battle raged more fiercely than ever. I had fired not less than eighty rounds, and only a few cartridges remained. Others had nearly exhausted their ammunition. At this point, to our great joy, we saw a line of battle advancing to our support. Steadily, quietly, they came on, their battle-flags gleaming through the trees, moving as orderly as if on dress-parade. As they neared us they quickened their pace, and charged forward with a tremendous cheer. It was a grand sight as they swept on, every eye fixed on the smoking timber beyond. But the little stream threw them into disorder, and they went rushing over the field without waiting to re-form. As they went over the rising ground which lay between them and the enemy, they received a terrible volley. Half their number seemed to go down before it. Back they rolled in confusion, leaving the ground strewn with their dead and wounded. They came back to the narrow flat by the run. There, as by one impulse, they rallied and proceeded to reform their lines. Not a man shirked. While they were forming, we opened fire again, over and past them. This lasted but a few minutes, and they were ready to advance. Steadily, irresistibly, their line passed up the slope, into the woods, driving every thing before it.

Our ammunition wagons had now come up, and we procured a fresh supply. We immediately moved down the stream and crossed, to drive back the enemy and retake the ground lost at this point. Here the bank on the other side was abrupt, rising thirty or forty feet in a very short distance, when level ground, partly open and partly wooded, extended toward the west and north. On this steep bank we formed for the charge, three lines of battle. The right of the regiment was detached, and placed on the left of the lines of battle to cover the flank. When the advance was made we deployed at skirmish distance, at a right angle with the line, and moving in the same direction. In this advance, which was made about two in the afternoon, we that were on the flank did not fire a shot. We were not much exposed, though some bullets whistled around.

We finally reached a farm-house in the midst of a large plantation. Here we halted. We found some of our wounded abandoned by the enemy, who seemed to have disappeared from our front. . Perhaps the decisive battle might have been fought on this afternoon instead of the following day, by pushing the Fifth Corps across the White Oak Road on the right of the intrenched position of the rebels. The course followed was probably the safer one.

At first the house which we had reached seemed to be deserted; but a little later we found the family, husband, wife, and daughter, concealed in a cave in the garden. The man was a tall, gray-haired old gentleman, all of them well dressed and evidently intelligent and refined people. The old man was so frightened that he could scarcely speak. They seemed to expect brutal treatment from the barbarians of the North, who, as it happened, were quite their equals in culture and humanity.

About five in the evening General Bartlett's brigade of the First Division was sent across the country to threaten the flank of the enemy, who had now pressed Sheridan back to Dinwiddie Court-house. They marched out past us toward the south-west, and disappeared from sight.

Darkness soon came on, and we prepared to pass another night under arms. It had been a hard day. We had lost eighteen hundred men, and inflicted a loss of one thousand on the enemy. Our losses fell chiefly on the Second and Third Divisions. Since ten o'clock the struggle had been almost continuous, and night found the enemy foiled in his purpose of driving us from our advanced position, which we now held more firmly than ever; but this was all the gain for either side. Some time after dark rations were distributed, and we lay down to sleep.

All the accounts of this battle that have come under my notice contain statements which I am not able to explain, if they are correct. It is generally stated that the corps

advanced toward the White Oak road, the
Second Division in front, the Third next, and
the First in the rear; that the Second Division was driven back on the Third, both on
the First, and that all were forced back to or
beyond the Boydton road. From the preceding narrative it will be seen that this was not
true of the right of the corps. When we
were compelled to fall back, in the forenoon,
we did not retreat more than three or four
hundred yards. The point at which we rallied
must have been fully half a mile from the
plank-road. If the rest of the corps did not
make a stand until they reached the plank-
road, it is rather surprising that a rebel force
was not thrown across the run on our left, by
which we would have been flanked and driven
away or captured. The run was a favorable
position for defense, while the vicinity of the
plank-road was not so good. Veteran soldiers
like those of the Fifth Corps would certainly
rally at the former point. It is probable that
some went back farther, while enough stopped
at the run to check the rebel advance. We
must have fought nearly three-quarters of an
hour before we were re-enforced. The troops
sent to our relief were from the Second Corps.

Chapter XVIII.

Pugnavimus ensibus.
We fought with our swords.
—Regner Lodbrog.

ABOUT midnight the Second Division was ordered down the plank-road to join Sheridan. Bartlett's brigade had proceeded as far as Gravelly Run, reaching it at dark. They found the stream swollen, the bridge gone, and the enemy strongly posted on the other side. The brigade was withdrawn during the night. It was no easy task to move troops under the circumstances. Orders had to go from corps commander down through brigade, regimental, and company officers to the privates, who had to be aroused from sleep and got into ranks without noise.

Through the deep mud and intense darkness we moved toward Dinwiddie Court-house. The darkness was so deep that we could tell nothing about localities. We must have marched past the Court-house. We might easily have passed the village without being aware of it. We then about-faced and retraced our steps for some distance. There is a road leads north from Dinwiddie toward Five Forks. We may have taken this, or we may have followed the plank-road a couple of miles farther back to a road which leads across to the one just mentioned. However this may be, daylight found us confronting the enemy somewhere in this vicinity. The only force found was a picket or skirmish line, which was easily driven away. The Second Division massed near the residence of J. M. Brooks, on the Five Forks road. Here we remained from about 7 A. M. until 10 A. M. During this time the other two divisions arrived, and took position a little north of us on the same road. When we reached this point the One Hundred and Ninetieth was thrown forward in skirmish line.

Meantime, the rebels had retired to their fortified position at Five Forks. Their works extended more than a mile, east and west, making a slight angle with the White Oak road, turning northward about a half-mile east of the Ford road. A heavy skirmish-line was deployed in front of their left, and extending some distance eastward, and south of the White Oak road. This force consisted of fourteen hundred riflemen, reputed the best in Lee's army. In this position they awaited our attack.

About ten o'clock we began to move, taking the road leading past Gravelly Run Church. At first there seemed to be some uncertainty about the movements and position of the enemy; but it was soon evident that his entire force was in our front. The column advanced along the road, with frequent brief halts, which indicated that we were nearing the foe. Erelong we could hear skirmishing, and an occasional discharge of cannon. Ambulances were passing, freighted with wounded cavalrymen, and later, stretcher-bearers, with their bloody burdens, met us, as we moved slowly toward the front.

Near Gravelly Run Church, our line of battle was formed. The Second Division was on the left, the Third on the right, the First in reserve, close behind the other two, a little on the right of the center. The two divisions in front were arranged as follows: Each division placed two brigades in front, in two lines each, and the remaining brigade in the rear of the center, in two lines. In the Second Division, the Maryland Brigade was on the left, ours on the right, and Winthrop's in reserve. The One Hundred and Ninety-first, including the fragment of the One Hundred and Fifty-seventh, and the Fourth Delaware, were the first line of battle, under Colonel Pattee. The One Hundred and Ninetieth was ordered forward to skirmish. We deployed in the woods, and waited for the completion of the arrangements going on in our rear. A few rods farther on there was open ground, which, in our front, gradually sloped down to woods. Opposite the left of the regiment, the open ground extended farther toward the north and west, and on that side was a slight hollow, with rough, broken ground beyond. Rebel skirmishers were in the woods in our front, now exchanging shots with cavalry in the open ground near us. Our skirmish-line was ready for business in a few minutes; but it was some time before the divisions were formed, in readiness for the assault.

If you should attempt to form an idea of that thin line of waiting men, who were to lead the way in the decisive struggle, which all knew was at hand, the mental picture would probably differ widely from the reality. Cast your eye to the left, along the line. You can see a goodly distance. The wood is not very dense. That does not look much like "battle's magnificently stern array." There is nothing magnificent or stern about it. You expected something of a scene. There is nothing of the sort. Instead, these men surprise you by their quiet bearing and seeming indifference. Most of them are young men. A few days ago they were so neat and tidy in dress and appearance, you might almost mistake that they were college students playing soldier. Now they are dirty, smeared with mud, half wet still from the rain, which only ceased this morning. Some are seated, leaning against the trees, taking it easy, conversing as pleasantly as if these were the ordinary occurrences of life. That bright-faced fellow, of Company E, is diligently polishing a little rusty spot, which he has discovered on his gun barrel. If there is time, he will scrape the mud from his shoes, and from his pants, which are stiff with it, almost to the knees. A few are nervous and anxious, but most of the really faint-hearted took advantage of the hard march last night to secure absence to-day. Dunn is on hand,—he that took himself from the field yesterday with such agility, at the beginning of the fight, and gave such comical reasons for his unceremonious flight, when he came up in the evening. R—— is in the line, looking black, silent, and still troubled in his knees. Do these careless men realize that they are about to decide the fate of a great nation? Perhaps they are unconscious of the greatness of the present hour; but what of that? They stood in their lot.

But our waiting is over at last; and, at the word of command, every soldier is in his place. These men were *not* stolid, ignorant, nor inexperienced. Their thinned ranks show how well they know what battle means. You can see some pale faces, and lips compressed, as "FORWARD" passes down the line. We pass out of the woods into the open field. A few rods ahead, some mounted cavalrymen are firing toward the woods, which conceal the enemy. We can see a puff of smoke here and there among the trees. A little farther, and the cavalry gallop away to the right, and bullets begin to whistle past, some over, some tossing up the dirt at our feet. It would be a waste of powder to return the fire at this distance; besides, we are going down there. But the bullets begin to come closer. They are fairly hot as they hiss around us. We quicken our pace. It is five hundred yards to the woods. The men on our left open fire—four hundred yards, three, the line slackens a little, and a volley, and another, and another, bursts in quick succession from our Spencer rifles. Then a cheer, as we dash for the woods at headlong speed, yelling and firing as we go. The rebel skirmishers give way before our charge, and the woods are gained.

Up to this time I had not looked back. I supposed we had advanced about a thousand yards, and would soon encounter the main force of the enemy. As we reached the woods, I turned to see if the line of battle was yet in sight. My eyes fell upon the most stirring scene I ever witnessed. This was the grandeur, the sublimity of war. The corps was coming in order of battle, line after line sweeping on with steady step. Their front extended nearly a mile across the open ground, guns at a right-shoulder, glittering in the sunlight like silver, battle-flags fluttering in the air. In front, the skirmishers were fighting savagely; on the left a score of cannon were thundering, shells screaming out their horrid warning, as they leaped from the smoking guns. But this living avalanche swept on in stern silence, as if there breathed within it a great soul, which scorned to speak or strike but once. A single glance took in the inspiring scene. I gazed but a moment, and then hurried into the woods.

The ground here consisted of alternate ridges and depressions, covered with trees and bushes, with occasional open places. It was hard ground to fight over, every ridge serving as a rallying point, and affording a superior position for defense. Our advance was now a succession of charges. When the rebels were driven from one ridge, they rallied at the next. A short distance from the edge of the woods, where we first encountered them, was a little brook, running nearly east; along its banks were some large rocks, while a few rods nearer were piles of wood, logs, and other means of shelter. Quite a large group of rebels made a stand here. Sergeant Hasler, Crocket, one or two others and myself, centered our attention on these, and advanced upon them, at first taking what cover we could among the trees, firing rapidly as we went. As we were pressing forward, my foot tripped on something, and I came to the ground with stunning force. Crocket, who was a few yards to my right, hurried toward me, his face the very picture of anxious sympathy, and inquired if I was struck. Recovering my breath, in a moment I was on my feet again, and assured him I was all right.

We now rushed on them with a cheer, and they broke and fled. We were so close on them, that seven of their number took refuge behind a large rock, while three or four more fled across the brook, leaving one of their number wounded on its bank. The men behind the rock now waved hats past it in token of surrender, and soon they were marching toward the rear in charge of Crocket. The wounded rebel whom I had seen fall, lay about a rod to the left, shot through the thigh. I gave him a drink, filled my canteen, and went on.

We had now become scattered, and made our way onward without much regard to order or concert of action. For a while the two lines were mingled together in the underbrush, so that you scarcely knew which way to look for friend or foe. Sometimes I was with others, and again entirely alone. The woods resounded with the yells of the combatants and the crack of rifles, as the deadly fight raged along the line.

Passing through the corner of an open field, I noticed some rebels eight or ten hundred yards to the left and front in such a position that I could give them a flank fire, while just a short distance from me in the field was a stone pile. The temptation was too strong to be resisted. I repaired to the stone pile and opened on them. At the first shot they looked to see whence it came; the next, they dodged, and hugged close to their rifle-pit, and then discovering me, they returned the fire. Their first shots went wild, but they soon got the range, and began to strike the stone pile. I gave them a few parting shots from my Spencer, and went on into the woods.

The skirmishing continued at close range, as before. The rebels fought stubbornly from point to point. Their works seemed farther off than we expected, but the crisis must come soon. We had just passed over a ridge, and the rebels had made a stand among the timber beyond. A slight depression lay between us, down which a gully had been washed by the water. None of our men were in sight, but I could hear their firing in the brush, right and left.

Wishing to gain the timber beyond the gully, I started forward without waiting to recharge my rifle, which I had just fired. The trees which I wished to gain were not more than forty feet away, and the gully about half that distance. I had gone but a step or two when a rebel soldier rose to his feet in the gully, facing me, with rifle in hand. It was a groundhog case. As he rose, I rushed at him, aiming at his heart and calling on him to surrender. He instantly dropped his gun. It was all over in less time than it takes to pen this sentence. His gun was loaded and capped. We waited till the line of battle came up. As they pushed through the brush behind us, seeing a rebel soldier, a dozen rifles were leveled on us; but they saw how it was in time to withhold their fire. Leaving my prisoner with them, I started forward again.

We soon reached an abrupt rise of ground beyond which we could not advance. Before us was the left of the enemy's intrenched position. We had done our work. We had driven every thing before us, and others must face the storm now. Some kneeling, others lying flat on the ground, we continued to fire and waited for the line of battle. In a few minutes we could see them coming on through the woods. A short distance behind us was a small patch of swampy, boggy ground. As this was approached orders were given and executed as coolly as if on the parade ground. The portion of the line opposite the swamp folded back of the other toward the left, and when the ground was passed, went back to place again without the least delay or confusion.

As they moved up the bank upon which we were, a volley burst upon them before which they wavered and swerved backward a few paces, as here and there a man reeled and staggered or sank to the earth. There was no panic—not a back turned—only that instinctive shrinking which Life sometimes feels when Death unexpectedly thrusts out his ghastly face through the smoke of battle. A color-bearer sprang forward with the battle-flag. He halted beside me and rested the end of the flag-staff on the ground. He half-faced about toward the men. His voice rang out like a bugle blast, as he raised his arm and shouted:

"Here are your colors!"

The line responded with a yell as it sprang forward, and soon was wrapped in the sulphurous smoke of its volleys which it thundered against the foe.

As the line moved on, I stepped behind them and passed farther to the right, and again went out ahead. The "left wheel" which the corps made in this battle resulted naturally from the position of the forces engaged. If we had moved directly forward in the direction in which we started, only the left of the Second Division would have struck the rebel's works; but the men posted in their front, as they were forced back, retreated toward the north-west, and we naturally swung around in following them.

We were now in front of the Third Division, the rebels still contesting every foot of ground. We finally drove them across an open field about a hundred yards wide. A road was on our left; at least all the Bucktails in sight were on the right of the road. A house stood near the road next to the woods, out of which we had driven the rebels, who were now firing from the farther side of the field. We were crossing the field, and some had reached the woods beyond, when the line of battle came up by the house behind us and opened fire. We hurried back to escape their bullets, which we considered more dangerous than those of the enemy. I stood behind them near the house, watching their firing, very much disgusted with the performance. There was a young lady in the house, apparently the only occupant. She was almost wild with fright, and gave vent to her feelings in screams and cries of terror.

A little lieutenant was prancing around back of the line, flourishing his saber in gallant style. He accosted me, and demanded why I was standing back, doing nothing. I replied that I did not belong on his — line, and made some comments perhaps not strictly polite. This added wrath to his excitement. I think this must have been the first time he had smelled gunpowder, except at a distance, and he supposed they were doing grandly. There was no telling how much effort it had cost him to get his courage screwed up sufficiently to bring him thus far; and to have this dirty, mud-bedraggled scrub of a boy intimate that the whole outfit should be furnished with long ears, was too much. As Homer would say, "his diaphragm became black all over." At this point Captain Birkman appeared on the scene and announced that he was responsible for me. This ended the matter.

After firing awhile, this brigade started to advance across the field. The regiment on the left moved up in good order as far as the edge of the woods. The others straggled forward in disorder. Both officers and men seemed to be confused. By the time they reached the woods they were little better than a mob, and had to halt to re-form. I think the man in command of the brigade was responsible for this. I now started out to skirmish again, intending to keep in front of the regiment on the left. As I reached the point where the road entered the woods, I met Mike Coleman coming on a run, and greatly excited.

"Why, Mike, I thought you were kilt! I heard you were shot in the head back yonder."

Scarcely pausing for a reply, he went on:

"We've got them! we've got them!

We're right in their rear. We'll take them all! Why don't these men come on?"

With this he hurried back to the men just behind us, and in a breath told them the situation, and urged them to come on without delay. To his great disgust, his appeals were unheeded, and he turned to me saying we would go alone. But now we saw some of the Bucktails coming forward, and soon about twenty of us were deployed at skirmish distance, advancing on the rebel rear. Their line could be seen stretching far to right and left. Our Spencers rattled among the trees as we rained the bullets upon them. They turned on us savagely, and their rifles blazed and flashed in reply. Presently their fire slackened. They right-faced, and began to move off toward the west, at first with some order; but soon they were only a panic-stricken mob, fleeing in all directions, some to the right, some to the left, others toward us. The latter we disarmed and sent to the rear without any guard, and kept up a fire on those who were running to the right. They threw down their guns by hundreds, and surrendered.

Toward the close a rebel soldier came

toward me at full speed, with his gun at a trail-arms. I did not notice him until he was within twenty-five or thirty yards of me. I yelled at him to surrender; but he came on without checking his speed. I stepped from the tree by which I was standing, and leveled my rifle on him.

"Drop that gun!" I yelled again.

He dropped it as if it had burned him, and hustled off his accouterments, and threw them on the ground. I made him stay with me, intending to take him back myself. My cartridges were about exhausted, and I fired all but one or two at the rear of the fleeing rebels, and started back with the prisoner.

The sun had now gone down. The moon was shining peacefully. How quickly those fateful hours of battle had passed! I started for the point where our line had formed, expecting to dispose of my prisoner there, and then sleep all night. As we passed along, the dead lay scattered here and there as they fell. There was something startlingly solemn in those motionless forms, the stony eyes staring in the moonlight.

Beyond the church I found a large number of prisoners, and turned over my man to the guards, and started to return. I was joined by L. C. Walb, who had also been back with prisoners. The church had been turned into a hospital. It was full of wounded, and many were laid on the ground outside. A few rods past the church we lay down to sleep. There came a reaction after the excitement of the day. Nerves, strained to their utmost tension for hours, relaxed, and seemed to tingle with the pain of weariness. The jarring noises of battle were reproduced as the senses glided through that strange interval between waking and sleeping, and more than once I came back to consciousness with a start, scarcely able, for a moment, to distinguish the real and the unreal. A low, moaning sound came from the hundreds of wounded about the church; not any single groan or cry of pain, but only a sound as if the hurried breath from suffering lips smote upon the strings of an unseen harp, which sounded out its sad cadences through the air. But at last I sunk into a sound sleep.

Our losses were less severe than on the preceding day. Eight hundred and thirty-four were killed and wounded, and fifty-four were missing. The opposing force of the enemy was practically annihilated. Three thousand were killed and wounded, and five thousand five hundred were made prisoners. Eleven stand of colors were taken, and four guns, with their caissons; also wagons and other material.

Captain Birkman, of Company A, says of this battle, in an extract kindly furnished from his diary: "The most successful attack I ever witnessed." It was a decisive battle, and settled the fate of the Confederacy. Since leaving camp on the morning of March 29th, three days before, the Fifth Corps had lost nearly one-fourth of its number in battles.

In this engagement the direct assault was made by the Second Division, the other divisions swinging around on the enemy's left flank and rear. The Third Brigade first struck, and broke through the rebel works. Sergeant Huck, with the colors of the One Hundred and Ninety-first, was the first man across the rebel rifle-pits. Colonel Pattee, commanding the first line, was the first mounted officer across, and leaped his horse over the breastwork while the foremost of the assailants were crowding over. They found themselves in the midst of the panic-stricken rebels, who threw down their arms and surrendered in large numbers. The Maryland brigade struck the rebel position almost at the same time, and with like results. The division then passed on down along the rear of the rebel position, doubling them up rapidly, and driving them in confusion.

We have read how the infantry faltered, till General Sheridan led them to the charge. We venture the opinion that this is wholly imaginary. These two brigades moved upon the rebel works as steadily and swiftly as the nature of the ground would allow. General Sheridan's reputation does not need any artificial bolstering, least of all at the expense of deserving men and officers.

The arbitrary removal of General Warren from the command of the Fifth Corps was unknown to the soldiers until the following morning. We heard only expressions of surprise and disapproval. It must be a cause of regret to all fair-minded men, that he was not allowed to share in this grand success with the men whom he had so long commanded. He was held in high esteem by the private soldiers, who regarded him as a brave and skillful officer.

Chapter XIX.

THE battle of Five Forks was fought on Saturday. Sabbath morning the sun rose bright and clear. When we camped the night before, Walb and myself planned for a substantial night's rest. For the first time since breaking camp, on the night of March 28th, we unpacked our blankets and made a bed. It was after sunrise when we awoke. Far to the right we could hear the low grumble of artillery, sounding like the roar of distant thunder. Since four o'clock in the morning a great battle had been raging in front of Petersburg, from the Appomattox on the right, to Hatcher's Run on the left.

Without waiting for breakfast, we went on to find the regiment. They were camped not far from where the roads crossed which formed the famous "Forks." At an early hour we were in motion, toward the right, where heavy and continuous firing could be distinctly heard. We passed by the ground where we had fought the evening before. The rebel dead were strewn far and near, like sheaves of grain in a harvest-field, showing how destructive had been our fire. The One Hundred and Ninetieth was deployed on the flank, and moved parallel to the column, at skirmish distance, about two hundred yards from it.

After marching for some time in the direction of Petersburg, we bore to the left, and about noon we reached the South Side Railroad, near Southerland's Station, and marched some distance along it. Beyond the road we found strong rifle-pits, which the enemy had abandoned. During the day news reached us that the works in front of Petersburg had been taken, and there was general rejoicing. That night we bivouaced near the Appomattox River.

April 3d we moved, at eight in the morning. Some firing was heard on our left, and many prisoners met us as we marched along. We found cannon abandoned in the road, and there was evidence on every hand that the rebels were hard pressed. Our general course was along what is called the river road, though we did not follow it all the time. Our movements and progress had to be governed by the supposed movements of the enemy. At one time we were deployed as skirmishers, and went down to the river. I do not know the reason of this precaution, but no enemy was found. We camped that night along the road.

April 4th we resumed the march, soon after sunrise. We were short of provisions, and foragers were sent out to secure what could be gathered from the country. I was out in the afternoon. While returning in the evening, after sun-down, I was shot at by some one, when quite near the column. That night we reached the Danville Railroad, near Jettersville, and camped in order of battle, about three miles from Lee's army. For this reason no fires were made. We had been thrown between him and Danville, which he was aiming to reach. Here Lee made a mistake. It was his duty to know of our presence here during the night. He should have attacked us promptly by daylight on the following morning; and, if possible, overwhelmed us before the rest of the army could arrive. There was little if any force confronting him, except the Fifth Corps, not more than twelve thousand men. I think we reached Jettersville in advance of the main body of the cavalry.

The morning of the 5th found us intrenched, and expecting an attack from the enemy. Rebel troops could be seen in the distance, and we supposed they were forming for battle. We stood behind the works waiting. Their skirmishers advanced and opened fire on our outposts. Hour after hour passed. At length the Second and Sixth corps arrived, and Lee's opportunity was lost.

April 6th we advanced, at first with some caution. But Lee was in full retreat toward Lynchburg, and we followed. During the day, a body of rebel cavalry made a dash at the wagon train, and we were ordered back to drive them off. We went back about three miles at double-quick. We met quite a number of men who had been skulking with the train, now rushing for the front at full speed. As we witnessed their consternation, we were entirely reconciled to the loss of a few wagons, just to see the "coffee brigade" shaken up. The rebels had been repulsed by our cavalry before we reached the scene. We remained with the train, and camped with it during the night. We marched twenty-nine miles, and arrived within five miles of High Bridge.

On the 7th we still remained with the train.

We passed a place where a rebel wagon train had been attacked by our cavalry. Ammunition and stores of all kinds were strewn everywhere. Wagon loads of shells had been emptied out, and lay scattered through the woods.

Some time during the day, we had halted by the road, and, as our rest was quite prolonged, some of the men had fallen asleep. Among others, Captain Birkman was sleeping soundly, perhaps dreaming of the peace that was now almost conquered. The woods were burning, a few rods on our right. The fire at last reached a lot of shells, which had been thrown from the wagons, to keep them from falling into the hands of the Yankees. They went off with a frightful clatter. The captain bounced from the ground as if a hornet had lifted him. "Fall in!" he shouted, grasping his sword. Of course, all who were awake comprehended the situation, and prudently lay still, to avoid the flying fragments. As the truth dawned upon him, the captain at first looked "sold" and disgusted, and then joined in the general laughter.

We halted that night near Prince Edward's Court-house, after a march of eighteen miles. Here we rejoined the brigade.

April 8th we made the most trying march of all. We lost some time by going out of the way, and made frequent halts during the forenoon, as if uncertain of the direction, or suspicious of the movement of the enemy. About noon we reached Prospect Station, thirteen miles from Farmville. In the afternoon we settled down to hard marching. We did not halt for supper. The sun went down, night came on, and still we marched on. By nine o'clock conversation had ceased—no breath could be wasted in words. Even "Sport" could no longer muster spirit to crack a joke on any body. You could only hear the "tramp, tramp" of feet, and the occasional clatter of a saber. But there was no grumbling. We knew this was the last forced march. One more blow, and treason would be crushed in the dust. As the column, from time to time, became clogged by some obstruction ahead, and halted for a moment, the men would sink down on the ground, most of them just where they stopped, to catch brief rest for their aching limbs. At such times I would be sound asleep in a moment, and more than once the column was marching on and myself with it when I awoke.

The Last Day.

Midnight came. and still we pressed on relentlessly. About one in the morning we saw lights ahead, which indicated that a halt had been made. Never did rest and sleep seem sweeter, nor a mile seem longer. It required a distinct effort of the will to compel each single step. But at last the task was accomplished. We had marched forty-two miles since sunrise, and lay within striking distance of the enemy.

The company was represented by Dunn, Bovard, Mike Coleman, Sergeant Hasler, and myself. The rest had broken down under the terrible strain and fallen behind. Without removing any thing, I threw myself on the ground, and knew no more until I was aroused at daylight to go on.

Just after sunrise we halted—for breakfast, they said. It was rather a grim sort of a joke. Scarcely one in fifty had any thing to eat. A few had coffee, and fires were made, and we went through the regulation motions of getting breakfast. This done, we started on again.

It soon became evident that the enemy had been brought to bay. The confused noise of battle rang through the air. We had halted in the woods, and stood in the road waiting, sure that the end had come.

Colonel Pattee was on his horse, half faced about toward his men, evidently impatient and eager. An aid gallops up with orders. Colonel Pattee looks happy. He gives his old horse an extra jerk:

"FORWARD! DOUBLE QUICK! MARCH!"

On we go toward the scene of conflict.

Again Colonel Pattee's voice rings out: "DEPLOY SKIRMISHERS!" and in less than a minute a line of Bucktails stretches through the woods, facing the enemy. There is no waiting. "FORWARD!" passes down the line, and we move out into the open field in front. A hundred yards ahead the cavalry are stubbornly facing a heavy force of rebel infantry that is crowding on them and steadily pushing them back. Now and then a man falls from his horse or rides back wounded. We were on lower ground than they, and the bullets whistled above us; but as we went up the rising ground, they began to hiss around our heads. We double-quicked forward and began firing.

Between us and the town there was a hollow, and on the farther ridge a road led down through the village. There was a wood on the left at the head of the hollow, and on the right a narrow strip of timber ran up to within two hundred yards of the road. The right of the regiment extended past the woods, or rather only a small portion of the left would strike them in moving straight forward. As we came to the ridge overlooking the hollow, we saw the rebel troops drawn up on the opposite slope. Soon they gave way and moved off toward the town out of sight, and a battery from the ridge opened with shell.

As soon as the battery opened fire, Robbins, myself, and two or three others started toward it. A rail fence ran along the hollow proper on the side next to us. As we neared the fence, Robbins, who was a few steps in advance, stopped.

"We had better stay here," he said, as he deliberately aimed at the battery.

"There are rebels in the woods there," meaning on the left. As he spoke, a bullet from the left clipped close over his gun barrel.

"See that!" he added, his aim not in the least disturbed. The gunners were shooting over us, as we supposed, at the line of battle farther back. But we had only fired a few shots when a shell burst in front of us, its fragments scattering dirt, fence rails, and splinters for yards around.

"Well! I think we'll go on," said Robbins. On we went to the farther side of the hollow, and under shelter of the bank, we kept up our fire with good effect. We would dodge their shells as they fired, and then rise and fire till they were ready again. Some riflemen in the vicinity of the battery gave us trouble, but failed to hit any of us.

After this had continued for some time, the One Hundred and Fifty-fifth Pennsylvania, a Zouave regiment, came down behind us on a double-quick, deployed as skirmishers. As they neared the fence a shell from the battery screamed over our heads, and exploding, killed one of their men. They heeded this no more than if it had not occurred, and came on with a cheer. Giving a parting shot to the battery which was now pulling out, we started on, bearing to the right toward the town. As we neared the point of the strip of woods on our right, Ginter, of Company E, stopped and sat down flat on the ground, remarking that it was getting mighty hot. I was of the same opinion, and halted a few feet in advance of him and fired a few shots in a kneeling posture. While thus engaged, I heard the sound of a blow behind me, and looking around, I saw Ginter tumbling on the ground, his heels in the air. He quickly gathered himself up to a sitting posture with a very rueful countenance, giving vent to his feelings in sundry expletives, as soon as he could get breath enough to deliver them properly. With many a doleful grunt he examined the extent of his injuries. A bullet had struck the belt of his cartridge-box, nearly over the heart. The ball had force enough almost to pierce the leather belt and severely bruise the chest, raising a lump half as large as a hen's egg, and very painful. Some fellow off to the left had reached for us, and well-nigh finished Ginter. He did not go to the rear, but kept on, holding his clothing from the painful bruise, too much engaged in this to do any more shooting.

A few minutes later, a rebel officer galloped along the line with a white flag. We were almost to the road at this time, at the outskirts of the town. We did not think of continuing the fight any longer, but some rebel soldiers on the left past the town, fired on us when we exposed ourselves, and we returned the treacherous fire, and advanced across the road. By the road, facing us as we approached, stood a negro cabin, out of which a rebel officer came as we reached it. A few words were exchanged between him and Adjutant Wright, and I think he was allowed to go down the road to where the main body of the rebel troops had halted. Our fire continuing, Colonel Pattee rode up to us, excitedly, to learn what it meant. Adjutant Wright explained that rebel skirmishers were still firing at us.

"Have this firing stopped at once," he said; and seeing a protest in Wright's face, he went on: "I tell you, you're excited, adjutant, and the men are excited. They've surrendered, and this must cease."

"Excited!" was the reply. "If they want to surrender, let *them* cease firing."

At this moment a bullet whizzed past the colonel's head, and killed a cavalry man on the bank beyond him. He rode off to the right, and left us to manage it to suit ourselves. In a little while the firing from both sides ceased. The Army of the Potomac had accomplished its mission. We had fought our last battle. The One Hundred and Ninetieth and One Hundred and Ninety-first had proved themselves, to the last hour, worthy successors of the Pennsylvania Reserves.

The preceding narrative will be better understood by a fuller statement of the part taken by the entire regiment in the engagement. The original intention was for Colonel Pattee to connect the right of his command with the First Division and the left with the command of General Ord. On reaching the front, he discovered that the cavalry were hard pressed, and would soon be dislodged from the woods, which would have to be regained at great disadvantage, and perhaps serious loss. He, therefore, ordered the regiment forward to their relief. Advancing rapidly, they relieved the cavalry and engaged the enemy before the troops on either flank were in position. Colonel Pattee now found his skirmish line confronting heavy lines of battle, and back of these, on the ridge near the village, in position to sweep all the open ground in front, Lee's artillery was massed. He at once thinned the exposed center and right of his line, strengthened the left, and charged boldly forward upon the enemy, throwing his left around upon their flank. Meantime the right pressed rapidly on, and engaged the rebel infantry in the open ground, and, later, the artillery on the ridge. Their infantry was routed, and driven back over the ridge, where their officers tried in vain to rally and lead them forward. Their artillery resisted with desperation until their commander was killed. By this time many of their horses had been shot, and they tried to drag the guns away by hand. But now the left of the regiment, under Colonel Pattee, came charging down on their right flank, bursting upon them like a tornado; and literally mingled together, almost fighting hand to hand, they went pell-mell toward the village. Here the flag of truce met them, and soon hostilities ceased. Rarely has a more brilliant and successful attack been executed in modern warfare, and it reflects the highest credit upon Colonel Pattee and his command. Rebel officers who witnessed it spoke in the highest terms of the splendid and reckless courage with which this skirmish line dashed upon the heavy masses of the enemy.

The death of the cavalryman, to which

reference has been made, was a cause of great regret to all who witnessed it. He was a brave young man. When relieved by the Bucktails, he might have retired from the field with honor, as did most of the command to which he belonged. He preferred, however, to remain. Falling in with Colonel Pattee, he fought by his side during all the engagement, charged with him in the last deadly onset, and escaped unharmed, to fall by the bullet of a cowardly truce-breaker.

Lieutenant Hayden, of the One Hundred and Ninety-first, a brave young officer, formerly of the Eleventh Reserves, lost a leg in this battle. It seemed hard to suffer death or maiming in this, the last hour, let us hope, that the nation will know of civil strife; but let us honor the men who were thus faithful to the end.

Chapter XX.

GENERALS GRANT, Meade, Ord, and others came down the road to the village. General Lee and his associates came in the opposite direction. They met at a house about two hundred yards from us, in full view of the place where we stood. Here the surrender was completed.

Twenty-six thousand men were surrendered. Besides those who had straggled and scattered through the country, or willfully deserted, Lee had lost in battle, since March 29th, 25,750 men. Both armies were much exhausted, and if Lee could have shaken off the clutch of Sheridan, and continued his retreat to Lynchburg, Grant would have been compelled to abandon the pursuit within three days, from lack of food for his army.

As soon as a few wagons came up with provisions, rations were issued to both armies; but there was not a sufficient supply. We remained on the skirmish line till the 10th, when we returned to the brigade. Several days of wet weather followed, and the wagon-trains could not be brought up. On the 15th we began the homeward march with empty haversacks.

We camped that night at Pamplin's Station. In the evening George Dunn stole a couple of the meanest, most diminutive, runty little hams you ever saw. I helped him eat them, and am willing to bear a fair share of the blame; but a country that can produce such hams needs reconstruction. On the 16th we reached Farmville. The next day we camped eight miles from Burksville. At the latter place we rested a few days, before resuming the march to Washington. Here the news first reached us of Lincoln's assassination. A number of men, who had been taken prisoners during 1864, rejoined us.

I was at headquarters one evening, for some purpose, when a soldier accosted me and inquired for the One Hundred and Ninetieth. He was ragged, thin, and pale. His hair and beard were of long growth. Looking into his haggard face and sunken eyes, there was not an outline I could recognize.

"The One Hundred and Ninetieth is right here. I belong to it."

"Are there any of Company D of the Eleventh Reserves here?"

"Yes; I belonged to Company D."

"You did!"

He leaned toward me, looked intently a moment, then reached out his hand.

"Why, Mac; I'm glad to find you."

As his face brightened I recognized him. It was Wm. Kenedy, of the old company. He was made prisoner May 5th, in the Wilderness. He had escaped from prison, and made his way through the country to our lines, traveling by night, hiding by day, fed by the slaves, nursed by them through a fever contracted in the swamps. Rest, food, and clean clothes soon made him look like himself again.

But my narrative must hasten to a close. We resumed the march, passed through Petersburg, Richmond, Fredericksburg, and camped at last on Arlington Heights. We participated in the grand review. It was something of more than ordinary interest, to see and compare the two great armies. Most of Sherman's army had but just arrived, and were dusty and travel-worn; while the army of the Potomac had been resting for some time, and looked fresher and more sprightly. The latter wore caps, and the former hats, which gave them a more somber appearance. I was also of the impression that there were more young men in our army than in Sherman's.

June 28th we were mustered out, and started the next day for Harrisburg, where we were discharged, July 2d.

The report of the Adjutant-general of Pennsylvania gives these two regiments, the One Hundred and Ninetieth and One Hundred and Ninety-first, no credit for active service subsequent to the battle of Welden Railroad, August, 1864. At this time, Colonel Carle, of the One Hundred and Ninety-first, and Colonel Hartshorn, of the One Hundred and Ninetieth, were made prisoners, with the greater part of their respective commands, and remained in captivity till after the cessation of hostilities. The remainder of the two regiments acted together as one organization, under command of Colonel Pattee, as mentioned on page 118, until the close of the war. This was by far the longest and most brilliant period of their history; but of this, the public records of the State make no mention. At the time of the muster out, Colonel Pattee was absent, and the report of the One Hundred and Ninetieth was made out by, or under the supervision of, Colonel Hartshorn; that of the One Hundred and Ninety-first by Colonel Carle. We suppose that these officers neglected to insert the names of the engagements which occurred while Colonel Pattee was in command.

The following is a list of the battles in which the regiment took part:

WHITE OAK SWAMP, .. { 190th, 191st, } Col. J. B. Pattee.
June 13, 1864,

PETERSBURG, ... { 190th, 191st, } Col. J. B. Pattee.
June 17, 1864,

WELDON RAILROAD, .. { 190th, 191st, } Col. W. R. Hartshorn. Col. —— Carle.
August 19, 1864,

The two colonels in command, with the greater part of their men, were made prisoners in this battle, after a heavy loss of killed and wounded.

2D WELDON RAILROAD, { 190th, 191st, } Captain Birkman.(?)
August 21, 1864,

POPLAR GROVE, ... { 190th, 191st, } Col. J. B. Pattee.
September 29, 1864,

HATCHER'S RUN, ...
October 27, 1864,   "   "   "   "

ROWANTY CREEK, ..
February 5, 1865,   "   "   "   "

HATCHER'S RUN, ...
February 6, 1865,   "   "   "   "

GRAVELLY RUN, ...
March 31, 1865,   "   "   "   "

FIVE FORKS, ...
April 1, 1865,   "   "   "   "

APPOMATTOX COURT-HOUSE,
April 9, 1865,   "   "   "   "

MAJOR R. M. BIRKMAN.

MAJOR R. M. BIRKMAN was born in St. Louis in April, 1837, and spent his childhood and early life in Harrisburg, Penn. He was in Philadelphia when the war was inaugurated by the firing on Fort Sumter, and at once enlisted in Company E, Eleventh Pennsylvania Reserves. He was made first sergeant, then commissioned second lieutenant, then promoted to first lieutenant, and after the reorganization, to captain of Company A, One Hundred and Ninetieth Pennsylvania.

At the close of the war he received the rank of brevet major for meritorious service. The following extract shows the esteem in which he was held by the officers with whom he was associated. It is from a letter of Brevet Brigadier-general Gwyn, who commanded the brigade in which he served during the latter part of the war:

"Captain, it affords me pleasure to testify to your bravery, ability, and universal good conduct in the several bloody fights in which your regiment was engaged during the late campaign. In the camp, no less than in the field, your conduct bore testimony to your worth. Sober, steady, and industrious, you set an example worth following."

In the army, as elsewhere, he was the quiet, unassuming, conscientious gentleman, doing his duty.

After the war, he returned to Blairsville, Penn., where he married Miss Mary L. Black, a most estimable lady of that city. He purchased the Blairsville *Press*, and continued to be editor and publisher of that paper till 1870. He then bought the *Indiana Register* and *American*, and merged the two papers into the *Indiana Progress*, which he published until the 1st of March, 1880. His health had been gradually failing for three or four years previous to this date; but he continued to devote his attention to the work which he loved, until the advance of disease warned him that his work was done. He then "set his house in order," fearlessly committed himself to the God whom he had served and loved, and waited calmly for the last of earth.

As death drew near, his mind went back over the scenes of camp and field, and he fought his battles o'er again. He died April 24, 1880. For seven years previous to his death he had been an active member of the

Presbyterian Church, and proved himself an earnest, consistent Christian.

BRIGADIER-GENERAL JOSEPH B. PATTEE.

BREVET BRIGADIER-GENERAL JOSEPH B. PATTEE is a native of Vermont. Of his life previous to the breaking out of the war we have no information. When the Pennsylvania Reserves were organized in 1861, he was commissioned first lieutenant Company B, of the Tenth. December 10, 1862, he was promoted to captain. At Bethesda Church, May 30, 1864, he was wounded in the knee by a grape-shot. He continued on duty, however, although this wound troubled him for more than a year afterward. When the reorganization took place, he was commissioned lieutenant-colonel of the One Hundred and Ninetieth Pennsylvania. Colonel Hartshorn being absent, he took command of the regiment. June 17th, he was severely wounded during the assault on Petersburg. A rifle-ball struck him in the center of the chest, and came out under his arm. This wound compelled an absence of nearly three months. He returned September 13th, although still suffering from this wound and the one received in May. During his absence, Colonel Hartshorn and Colonel Carle, of the One Hundred and Ninety-first, returned, and took command of their respective regiments. These officers, with the greater part of their men, were made prisoners August 19th, and so remained until after the cessation of hostilities.

The remainder of the two regiments, increased during the Fall by returning convalescents, numbered about five hundred men. Colonel Pattee took command of these, and they acted together as one organization. To his care, skill, and courage they owe the brilliant record which they made during the rest of their history. At Gravelly Run his promptness and decision saved the Union forces from serious disaster. His gallant conduct in leading the assault on the rebel intrenchments at Five Forks is mentioned in the account of that battle. At Appomattox Court-house he was ordered forward with his regiment from the rear of the division, for the purpose of making that last dash against Lee, and compelling his surrender. For the prompt and skillful manner in which this attack was executed, he was highly complimented by the generals in command, and was brevetted brigadier-general.

Since the close of the war he has been in the West, and is now engaged in a land agency business at Canton, Dakota Territory.

THE following muster-rolls are obtained from the "History of the Pennsylvania Volunteers." The roll of Company C, One Hundred and Ninetieth, is defective in that work, and we have added a few names from memory. The following abbreviations need explanation: M. A. C. D. C. = Military Asylum Cemetery, District of Columbia; V. R. C. = Veteran Reserve Corps; N. C. = National Cemetery. The date which follows the name and rank of an officer, or the name of a private, indicates the date of enlistment.

Company C, 11th P. R. V. C.

MUSTERED OUT JUNE 13, 1864.

- S. Louden, Capt.; June 10, '61; disc. sur. cer., Sept. 26, '62.
- W. H. Timblin, Capt.; June 10, '61; Brev. Maj.; wounded in Wilderness; must. out with Co.
- Newton Redic, 1st Lt.; June 10, '61; killed at Gaines' Mill, June 27, '62.

G. W. Fliger, 1st Lt.; June 10, '61; pris. May 5, '64; disc. March 12, '65.

J. C. Kuhn, 2d Lt.; June 10, '61; died of wounds, Sept. 17, '62.

J. H. Sutton, 2d Lt.; June 10, '61; disc. for wounds, July 3, '63.

W. J. Halderman, 1st Sergt.; Oct. 1, '61; trans. 190th, vet.

G. W. Milford, Sergt.; June 10, '61; disc. sur. cer., Jan. 20, '63.

J. H. Christie, Sergt.; June 10, '61; killed at Gaines' Mill, June 27, '62.

G. A. Black, Sergt.; June 10, '61; must. out with Co.
J. T. Kelly,   "   "   "   "   "   "
G. W. Eby,   "   "   "   "   "   "
M. Heckart,   "   "   "   "   "   "

W. Prior, Sergt.; June 10, '61; pris. May 5, '64; died at Andersonville, Nov. 28, '64; grave 12,191.

Hiram Black, Corp.; June 10, '61; died of wounds, Dec. 18, '62.

J. W. Campbell, Corp., June 10, '61; must. out with Co.
S. Cook,   "   "   "   disc. on sur. cer.
J. H. Meeder,   "   June 23, '61;   "   "   "

R. S. Harper, Corp.; Feb. 24, '62; trans. 190th; disc. Feb. 24, '62.

J. S. Campbell, Corp.; June 10, '61; pris. May 5, '64; disc. Dec. 22, '64.

R. S. Ray, Corp.; June 10, '61; must. out with Co.
W. P. Black, "   "   "   "   "   "
J. M. Varnum, mus., "   "   "   "   "
J. Heckart,   "   June 23, '61;   "   "   "

PRIVATES.

Allen, D. S.; June 10, '61; must. out with Company.
Adams, H. C.; Oct. 1, '61; disc. sur. cer., June 30, '62.
Anderson, R. M.; Mar. 4, '62; "   "   June 24, '62.
Birch, D.; June 10, '61; must. out with Company.
Black, J. R.; June 10, '61; pris. May 5, '64; disc. Dec. 12, '64.
Bell, S. M.; June 10, '61; disc. for wounds, May 20, '63.
Brandon, Henry; June 10, '61; disc. for wounds, Oct. 10, '62.
Beatty, S. R.; June 10, '61; disc. for wounds rec'd at Gaines' Mill.
Bryan, W. A.; June 10, '61; disc. on sur. cer., Feb. 11, 63.
Bruner, S.; June 23, '61; pris. May 5, '65, to Ap. 17, '65.
Black, U. J.; June 10, '61; died Dec. 26, '62; buried in M. A. Cem., D. C.
Beam, J.; June 10, '61; died Aug. 7, '62, of wounds rec'd at Gaines' Mill.
Brewster, J. C.; June 10, '61; died July 23, '62; buried in M. A. Cem., D. C.
Boreland, J. W.; June 10, '61; died May 22, '62.
Campbell, I.;   "   "   must. out with Co.
Christy, H. F.;   "   "   "   "   "
Cannon, J.; June 23, '61; absent, sick, at muster out.
Campbell, R. G.; Feb. 29, '64; trans. to 190th; pris., died at Andersonville, Aug., '64.
Campbell, Wm.; June 10, '61; died Aug. 1, '63, of wounds rec'd at Gettysburg; bur. N. C., sec. D., grave 39.
Clark, C.; died May 12, '65; bur. Cypress Hill Cem., Long Island.

Dobson, J.; June 10, '61; mort. wounded, May 30, '64.
Donaldson, J.; June 10, '61; pris. May 30, '64; disc. Dec. 16, '64.
Edgar, H. J.; June 23, '61; disc. for w'ds, Nov. 23, '62.
Eshenbaugh, J.; June 10, '61; trans. to 190th; pris., May 30, '64, to April 17, '65; must. out vet.
Fliger, E. S.; June 10, '61; disc. on sur. cer., Nov. 27, '61.
Fliger, Jacob; June 10, '61; disc. on sur. cer., Nov, 27, '62.
Graham, Jas. K.; June 10, '61; wounded; must. out with Company.
Grossman, Lewis; June 10, '61; wounded, with loss of arm and leg, May 11, '64; died Aug. 3, '64; bur. N. C., Arlington.
Hindman, R. S.; June 10, '61; must. out with Co.
Halstead, Jn.; June 23, '61; " " "
Hilliard, W.; " " " " "
Hilliard, W. H.; June 10, '61; disc. sur. cer., May 11, '62.
Henlen, Jn. D. W.; June 10, '61; disc. sur. cer., Jan. 8, '63.
Hoffman, Ed.: March 4, '62; trans. to 190th.
Hilliard, Eli; June 10, '61; died at Richmond, Jan. 11, '63, of wounds received at Fredericksburg.
Hyskill, G.; June 10, '61; killed at Fred., Dec. 13, '62.
Hart, Samuel; March 4, '62; died Aug. 10, '62.
Karner, Wm.; June 10, '61; must. out with Company.
Krause, R.; June 23, '61; pris. May 5, '64; disc. Mar. 1, '65.
Kepler, A. C.; Oct. 1, '61; w'd and pris. at Gaines' Mill; disc.
Kautch, Wolfgang; June 10, '61; disc. for wounds, Dec. 31, '63.

Muster-Rolls.

Kenedy, B. F.; Mar. 4, '62; trans. to 190th; disc. at expiration of term.

Larden, T. P.; June 23, '61; wounded at Fred.; pris. May 5; disc. Mar. 14, '65.

Linsay, F.; June 10, '61; died Jan. 4, '63, of wounds rec'd at Fred. Dec. 13, '62; bur. M. A. C., D. C.

Livermore, J.; Oct. 1, '61; trans. V. R. C., Dec. 31, '63.

Miller, S.; June 10, '61; pris. May 5, '64; disc. Mar. 5, '65.

M'Cleary, S. E.; June 10, '61; pris. May 5, '64; disc. Mar. 5, '65.

M'Gill, W. B.; June 10, '61; disc. on sur. cer., Dec. 30, '61.

Malarkey, D.; June 23, '61; disc. Feb. 11, '63.

Moore, W. E.; June 10, '61; disc. for w'ds, Sept. 1, '63.

M'Murry, S.; " " " " Dec. 3, '62.

M'Elhany, R.; " " " " " 29, '62.

M'Elvain, R.; " " " " Jan. 15, '63.

M'Call, Alex.; Feb. 8, '62; " " rec'd at Fred.

Milford, J. P.; Aug. 26, '62; trans. to 190th.

Monnie, F. H.; Sept. 21, '62; trans. to 190th; disc. at expiration of term.

M'Murry, R.; Feb. 8, '62; trans. to 190th; disc. at expiration of term.

M'Camy, J.; Feb. 24, '62; trans. V. R. C., Dec. 21, '63.

Miller, Isaiah: June 10, '61; died Aug. 13, '62; bur. at Point Lookout.

Martin, Wm.; Sept. 21, '61; died of w'ds. Sept. 17, '62.

M'Bride, W. A.; June 10, '61; killed at Gaines' Mill, June 27, '62.

Martin, P. G.; June 23, '61; deserted Mar. 20, '63.

Patterson, H. B.; June 10, '61; must. out with Co.

Pearce, J. M.; June 10, '61; disc. for w'ds, Oct. 29, '62.

Pearce, R. C.; Aug. 26, '62; died Dec. 13, '62; bur. M. A. C., D. C.

Pettigrew, A. J.; June 10, '61; died July 11, '63, of wounds rec'd at Gettysburg.

Porter, J. R.; Oct. 5, '61; died Sept. 25, '62, of w'ds rec'd at Bull Run, Aug. 30, '62.

Rhodes, G. M.; June 10, '61; disc. on sur. cer., Aug. 23, '62.

Rothmire, G.; June 10, '61; disc. Sept. 12, '62, for wounds rec'd at Gaines' Mill.

Rinker, Wm.; June 10, '61; disc. Sept. 12, '62, for wounds rec'd at Bull Run, Aug. 30, '62.

Russel, D. H.; Aug. 26, '62; trans. to 191st.

Rosenberry, J.; June 10, '61; died at Macon, Ga., Dec. 24, '62, of wounds rec'd at Fredericksburg.

Russel, O. H. P.; June 10, '62; died at Richmond, Dec. 31, '62, of wounds rec'd at Fredericksburg.

Sloan, Wm.; June 10, '61; must. out with Company.

Seaton, Amos; "   "   "   "   "

Shryock, S. P.; June 10, '61; pris. May 5, '64; disc. Mar. 5, '65.

Say, Hon. H.; Oct. 7, '61; trans. to 191st.

Stevenson, J. H.; June 10, '61; killed at South Mountain, Sept. 14, '62.

Schmidt, C.; June 10, '61; killed at South Mountain, Sept. 14, '62.

Shepard, J. M.; Sept. 21, '61; disc. for w'ds, Feb. 24, '63.

Taylor, J. L.; June 10, '61; must. out with Company.

Thompson, W. S.; June 10, '61; disc. on sur. cer., Aug. 2, '62.

Thompson, J.; Oct. 13, '61; killed at Gaines' Mill.

White, Allen; June 10, '61; killed at Wilderness, May 5, '64.

Company D, 11th P. R. V. C.

Wm. Stewart, Capt.; July 5, '61; w'nded 2d Bull Run; killed at Fredericksbug, Dec. 13, '62.

Jacob Baiers, Capt.; July 5, '61; disc. April 9, '64, for wounds received at Gaines' Mill.

Jas. P. Boggs, Capt.; July 5, '61; Brev. Maj.; wd. twice, pris. once, must. out with Co.

J. S. Kenedy, 1st Lt.; July 5, '61; disc. June 13, '63, for wds. received at South Mountain, Sept. 14, '62.

Jesse Donaldson, 2d Lt.; July 5, '61; died at Alexandria, Va., May 5, '62.

J. O'Harra Woods, 2d Lt.; July 5, '61; killed at Gettysburg, July 2, 63; N. C., sec. C., grave 35.

Wilson R. Potts, 1st Sergt.; July 5, '61; disc. sur. cer. June 10, '62.

Wm. C. Coleman, 1st Sergt.; Sept. 8, '61; trans. 190th to 1st Lt., Co. I; must. out June 28, '65.

Robt. Ash, Sergt.; July 5, '61; disc. sur. cer. June 10, '62.

Jn. Ganz, Sergt.; July 5, '61; must. out with Co.

Sam'l J. Chrisley, Sergt.; July 16, '61; killed at 2d Bull Run, Aug. 30, '62.

Jac. B. Kinsell, Sergt.; July 5, '61; died Jan. 20, '63; wounds received at Fred.; Alex. grave 691.

G. W. M'Gaughey, Sergt.; July 5, '61; died Rich. Feb. 10, '63, wounds received at Fred., Dec. 13, '62.

David C. Steen, Sergt.; July 5, '61; trans. 190th; wd. Gaines' Mill, Fred., Wild.; killed Weldon R. R., Aug. 19, '64., vet.

Geo. Weber, Sergt.; July 5, '61; wounded Fred.; pris. May 5, '64; disc. Dec. 17, '64.

Jas. M'Clelland, Sergt.; July 29, '61; must. out with Co.
Jas. M. Graves, Sergt.; July 12, '61; pris. May 5, '64; must. out Dec. 18, '64.
Jn. Dunbar, Corp.; July 5, '61; killed at Gaines' Mill, June 27, '62.
Silas Amberson, Corp.; July 5, '61; killed at Gaines' Mill, June 27, '62.
Robt. G. Gilleland, Corp; July 5, '61; disc. sur. cer., Feb. 4, '63.
David P. Stewart, Corp.; July 5, '61; killed at Gaines' Mill, June 27, '62.
David S. Parks, Corp.; July 6, '61; killed May 30, '64.
Jas. R. Moore, Corp.; July 29, '61; disc. on sur. cer., Feb. 7, '63.
Jas. B. Shafer, Corp.; July 29, '61; trans. 190th; must. out June 28, '65.
Dan'l Graham, Corp.; July 5, '61; pris. May 30, '64; died —.
Jesse Fry, Corp.; July 5, '61; must. out with Co.
Chas. Minnemyer, Musician; July 6, '61; promoted to prin. musc., Nov. 1, '63; must. out with Co.
Alf. Nixon, musc.; July 5, '61; must. out with Co.

PRIVATES.

Addleman, Lind. H.; Feb. 24, '62; died at home on Furlough.
Barron, Barn. C.; July 5, '61; disc. sur. cer., Aug. 3, '62.
Beers, Jn.; Feb. 8, '62.; trans. 190th; pris. Aug. 19, '64; not accounted for.
Berchtold, Jas.; Feb. 25, '62; trans. U. S. N., Nov. '62.
Beers. Sm'l; July 5, '61; trans. V. R. C., Sept. 1, '63.

Beggs, Jn.; July 5, '61; trans. V. R. C., Sept. 1, '63.
Beatty, Jn. M.; July 5, '61; killed at Gaines' Mill, June 27, '62.
Bedillion, Peter; July 16, '61; died Jan. 17, '62.
Beltz, Chas.; ———; died Sept. 4, '62; bur. Alexandria, grave 212.
Boggs, Wm.; July 5, '61; must. out with Co.
Brennamin, S.; March 18, '64; trans. 190th; pris. Aug. 18, '64; not accounted for.
Brown, Robt. J.; July 16, '61; trans. 190th; not accounted for.
Brown, Jn. M.; July 5, '61; must. out with Co.
Brunnermer, Geo.; Feb. 8, '62; trans. 190th; wd. May 30, Aug. 18, '64; must. out, vet.
Burr, Jacob; Feb. 25, '64; trans. 190th; pris. Aug. 19, '64; not accounted for.
Cartwright, Linas; July 16, '61; disc. sur. cer., March 1, '64.
Campbell, David; July 16, '61; disc. sur. cer., Aug. 28, 63.
Cowan, Jn.; July 5, '61; disc. sur. cer. ———
Corans, Jn.; Sept. 12, '61; trans. V. R. C., Sept. 1, '63.
Cress, Dan'l; July 29, 61; " " " "
Critchlow, A. W.; July 5, '61; died at N. Y., Oct. 2, '62.
Critchlow, J. W.; July 5, '61; killed at Gaines' Mill, June 27, '62.
Cornelius, T. J.; July 29, '61; killed at Gaines' Mill, June 27, '62.
Conders, Jn.; July 5, '61; killed at Bull Run, Aug. 30, '62.
Dodds, Jasper P.; July 12, 61; died at Richmond, July 18, '62, of wds. received at Gaines' Mill.

Dodds, W. F.; July 29, '61; disc. sur. cer., Oct. 7, '62.
Deer, Jac.; July 5, '61; disc. sur. cer., March 11, '63.
Divinney, J. G.; Sept. 21, '61; disc. sur. cer, May 9, '62.
Elliott, J. P.; July 5, '61; pris. May 5, '64; died —.
Fleming, T. H.; July 5, '61; trans. 190th; must. out with Co., June 28, '65, vet.
Frail, M.; July 5, '61; killed at Gaines' Mill, June 27, '62.
Fry, W. M.; July 5, '61; died at Washington, D. C., May 31, '62.
Graham, D. W.; Sept. 21, '61; disc. sur. cer., Aug. 18, '62.
Gilleland, R. S.; Feb. 10, '64; trans. 190th; pris. Aug. 19, '64; not accounted for.
Gilleland, W.; Feb. 10, '64; trans. 190th; pris. Aug. 19, '64; not accounted for.
Gilpatrick, M.; March 17, '64; trans. 190th; pris. Aug. 19, '64; disc. July 5, '65.
Gibson, Israel; March 17, '64; trans. 190th; pris. Aug. 19, '64; disc. July 5, '65.
Graham, D. W.; Aug. 19, '61; trans. V. R. C., Sept. 1, '63.
Greer, J. A.; July 5, '61; trans. V. R. C., Sept. 9, '63.
Hussleton, G. W.; July 5, '61; pris. May 5, 64; disc. Dec. 22, 64.
Haslett, S. F.; Sept. 10, '61; disc. sur. cer., Nov. 21, '62.
Haslett, J. B.; March 3, '62; trans. V. R. C., Sept. 1, '63.
Hare, Peter; July 12, 61; trans. 190th; pris. Aug. 19, '64; shot Salis., N. C., Dec. 22, '64, vet.
Hoyt, Oscar C.; Sept. 21, '61; trans. V. R. C., Sept. 1, '63.

MUSTER-ROLLS.

Johnson, J. B.; July 25, '61; died May 30, '62; bur. M. A. C., D. C.
Johnston, Vernon; July 5, 61; died July 9, '61.
Kenedy, Alex.; July 29, '61; disc. sur. cer., Feb. 9, '63.
Kenedy, W. H. H.; July 5, '61; trans. 190th; pris. May 5, '64; must. out June 28, '65, vet.
Kalb, Eckart; March 10, '62; trans. 190th; wd., loss of arm, May 30, 64.
List, Wm.; July 14, '61; must. out with Co.
Lyon, Sm. A.; July 24 '61; k. Bull Run, Aug. 30, '62.
Leonard, Jas.; July 5, '61; deserted Aug. 31, '61.
M'Nair, Robt. A.; July 5, '61; must. out with Co.
Mushrush, B. L.; July 5, '61; wd. May 5, '64; must. out with Co.
M'Donald, D. (1); July 5, '61; must. out with Co.
M'Donald, D. (2); July 16, '61; disc. sur. cer., June 25, '63.
M'Aleer, B. W.; Feb. 24, '62; trans. 190th; pris, Aug. 19, '64; not accounted for.
M'Bride, R. E.; Dec. 15, '63; trans. 190th; must. out June 28, '65.
M'Comb, J. H.; Feb. 9, '64; trans. 190th; pris. Aug. 19, '64; not accounted for.
Miller, Ed.; Feb. 25, '64; trans. 190th; must. out with Co., June 28, '65.
M'Curdy, S. R.; Sept. 8, '61; trans. to Co. B., May 1, '62; disc. sur. cer., June 4, '62.
M'Knight, J.; Sept. 12, '61; trans. V. R. C., Feb. 5, '64.
Moreland, C. L.; Apr. 22, '64; trans. 190th; killed at Petersb., June 24, '64; bur. in Poplar Grove Cem., grave 173, sec. C. div. D.
M'Cullough, M. F.; July 6, '61; killed May 5, '64.

Moore, Wm.; July 16, '61; killed at Gaines' Mill, June 27, '62.

M'Kinney, J. A.; July 5, '61; killed at Bull Run, Aug. 30, '62.

M'Neal, W. R.; Sept. 8, '61; died Oct. 25, '62, of wds. rec'd at Bull Run, Aug. 30, '62; bur. M. A. C., D. C.

Nixon, J. E.; July 6, '61; disc. sur. cer., March 28, '64.

Overdoff, W. C.; March 31, '64; trans. 190th; killed Oct. '64.

Parker, S. C.; July 5, '61; must. out with Co.

Pisor, D. W.; July 16, '61; died Nov. 16, '62; buried Camp Parole, Hospital Cem. Annapolis, Md.

Pherson, R. J.; July 29, '61; killed at Bull Run, Aug. 30, '62.

Rodgers, H.; July 16, '61; disc. sur. cer., June 23, '62.

Richardson, W.; March 21, '62; trans. 190th; wd. at Fred.; must. out June 28, '65, vet.

Robertson, J.; Feb. 16, '64; trans. 190th; pris. Aug. 19, '64; died —.

Rice, T. G.; Feb. 13, '64; trans. 190th; pris. Aug. 19, '64; died Dec. 23, '64, Salisbury, N. C.

Rosenberry, S. J.; Feb. 24, '62; died June 23, '62; bur. Mil. As. Cem., D. C.

Rouch, L.; Oct. 5, '61; died at home, Butler County, Sept. 8, '63.

Smith, S. F.; Sept. 8, '61; disc. sur. cer., Aug. 1, '62.

Shearer, W M.; Sept. 8, '61; disc. sur. cer., Aug. 27, '62.

Stevenson, B.; Feb. 24, '62; disc. sur. cer., March 25, '62.

Snow, Alf. M.; July 5, '61; trans. 190th; pris. Aug. 19, '64; died Salisbury, N. C., vet.

Shank, A.; Sept. 8, '61; trans. 190th; must. out June 28, '65., vet.

Shank, Jn.; Feb. 26, '64; trans. 190th; not accounted for.
Silvers, M.; Sept. 21, '61; trans. V. R. C.
Stanley, J. S.; March 31, '64; trans. 190th; wd. May 30, '64; not accounted for.
Sinott, Wm.; Sept. 8, '61; killed at Bull Run, Aug. 29, '62.
Summerville, J. H.; July 5, '61; died at Annapolis, Md., Feb. 28, '63, of wds. rec'd at Fred. Dec. 13, '62.
Teets, Al.; July 5, '61; absent at muster out.
Thompson, R. W.; July 5, '61; must. out with Co.
Thompson, G.; July 23, '61; "   "   "
Williamson, Hugh; July 5, '61; wd. at Fred.; absent at muster out.
Woods, Wm.; July 5, '61; died at Camp Pierpont, Dec. 6, '61.
Young, Geo.; Feb. 8, '62; disc. sur. cer., June 11, '62.

Company C, 190th P. V.

Neri B. Kinsey, Capt.; June, 1, '61; Brev. Maj. Oct. 1, '64; wounded Oct., '64; disc. Mar. 8, '65.
Moses W. Lucore, 1st Lt.; June 1, '61; pris. Aug. 19, '64; must. out June 28, '65.
Benj. F. Wright, 2d Lt.; pris. Aug. 19, '64; must. out June 28, '65.
—— Keeley, Sergt.; must. out June 28, '65.
—— Haslett, "   "   "   "   "
David C. Steen, Sergt.; killed Aug. 19, '64; sec. D., 11.
Thos. H. Lindsay, Corp.; Dec. 21, '63; disc. gen. ord., June 1, '65.

PRIVATES.

Brown, Robt. J. ; July 16, '61 ; vet., not accounted for.
Beers, Jn. ; Mar. 17, '62 ;   "   "   "
Burr, Jacob ; Feb. 25, '64 ;   "   "   "
Brunnermer, George ; Feb. 8. '62 ; ward 2 ; mus.
Brennamin, Sl. ; Mar. 18, '64 ; pris. Aug. 19, '64 ; not accounted for.
Bovard, Joseph O. ; June 8, '61 ; must. out with Co., June 28, '65, vet.
Conner, Wm. ; Sept. 22, '62 ; pris. Aug. 19, '64 ; disc. gen. ord., June 1, '65.
Coleman, Mike ; Dec. 15, '63 ; must. out with Co., June 28, '65.
Dunn, Geo. ; Sept. 22, '62 ; disc. gen. ord., June 1, '65.
Edgar, Jn. ; must. out with Co., June 28, '65, vet.
Eshelman, Abram ; Dec. 9, '63 ; died of wounds rec'd at Petersburg, Va., June 17, '64.
Fulkerson, Smith ; Mar. 31, '62 ; disc. at expiration of term.
Fleming, Thorn. H. ; July 5, '61 ; must. out with Co., June 28, '64, vet.
Fuller, Jn. A. ; pris. Aug. 19, '64 ; died at Salisbury N. C., Dec. 12, '65.
Fairbanks, D. ; pris. Aug 19, '64 ; died Nov. 24, '64.
Gilpatrick, Mark ; Mar. 15, '64 ; pris. Aug. 19, '64, to Oct. 8, '64 ; disc. July 5, '65.
Gilleland, Robt. S. ; Feb. 10, '64 ; not accounted for.
Gilleland, Wilson ;   "   "   "   "   "
Gibson, Israel ; Mar. 17, '64 ;   "   "   "
Hare, Peter ; July 12, '61 ; pris. Aug. 19, '64 ; died at Salisbury, N. C., Jan. 30, '65, vet.
Harris, Abram ; Feb. 3, '64 ; disc. gen. ord., May 16, '65.

Muster-Rolls. 245

Harris, Wm.; Feb. 3, '64; must. out with Co., June 28, '65.
Kalb, Eckart; Mar. 10, '62; wounded, with loss of arm, May 30, '64.
Kenedy, W. H. H.; July 5, '61; pris. May 5, '64; must. out with Company, June 28, '65, vet.
Klinglesmith, C.; Feb. 5, '64; must. out with Co., June 28, '65.
Lewis, Wm.; Oct. 25, '64; disc. gen. ord., June 5, '65.
Lyons, Owen; Dec. 21, '63; trans. V. R. C.
M'Aleer, Bernard W.; Feb. 24, '62; not accounted for.
M'Bride, R. E.; Dec. 15, '63; must. out with Co.
M'Comb, Jas. H.; Feb. 9, '64; pris. Aug. 19, '64; not accounted for.
M'Guire, Robt. R.; June 8, '61; mustered out with Company, vet.
M'Guire, Jas. N.; June 8, '61; must. out with Company, vet., wounded.
Miller, Ed.; Feb. 25, '64; must. out with Company.
Nicholson, Jn.; Dec. 31, '63; pris. Aug. 19, '64, to Feb. 7, '65; disc. June 12, '65.
Overdoff, Wm. C.; Mar. 31, '64; killed Oct., '64.
Payne, Wm.: Oct. 20, '61; disc. at expiration of term.
Rice, Thos. G.; Feb. 13, '64; pris. Aug. 19, '64; died at Salisbury, N. C.
Richardson, Wm.; Mar. 21, '62; must. out with Co., wounded.
Robertson, Jas.; Feb. 16, '64; pris. Aug. 19, '64; died at Salisbury, N. C., Dec. 23, '64.
Rutter, Wm.; wounded at Petersburg, June 18, '64; died July 15, '64.
Snow, Alf. M.; July 5, '61; pris. Aug. 19, '64; died at Salisbury, N. C., vet.

Shank, Andrew; Sept. 8, '61 ; must. out with Co., vet., wounded.
Shank, Jn.: Feb. 26, '64; not accounted for.
Scott, W. D.; June 8, '61 ; disc. Jan. 23, '65, vet.
Stohker, Abram; Dec. 21, '63; pris. Aug. 19, '64, to Jan. 23, '64; disc. June 12, '65.
Sweeney, Chas. ; June 8, '61 ; pris. Aug. 19, '64, to March 1, '65; disc. June 24. '65.
Thiel, Anthony ; Feb. 4, '62 ; disc. gen. ord., June 2, '65.
Walb, Leonidas C.; June 21, '61 ; must. out with Company, vet.
Youler, Benj. F.; June 20, '61 ; must. out with Co., vet.

GREAT WESTERN GUN WORKS, Pittsburgh, Pa.

Breech-loading Shot Guns, $18 to $300. Double Shot Guns, $8 to $150. Single Guns, $3 to $20. Rifles, $8 to $75. Revolvers, $1 to $25. Send for free illustrated Catalogue. Great Western Gun Works, Pittsburgh, Pa.

NEW EDITION. Contains 1928 Pages, 3000 ENGRAVINGS, 4600 New Words and Meanings, **Biographical Dictionary,** 9700 Names.

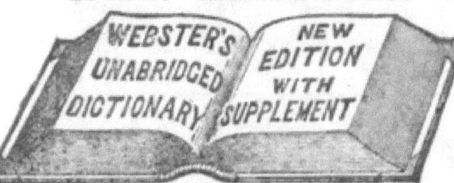

Published by G. & C. MERRIAM, Springfield, Mass.

Western Reserve Seminary,
WEST FARMINGTON, OHIO.

C. B. WEBSTER, A. M., Principal.

INSTITUTION ESTABLISHED FIFTY YEARS.
OPEN TO BOTH SEXES.

Five Departments in Successful Operation: Classical, Scientific, Commercial, Normal, Music, and Art Courses, Telegraphy, and Printing.

TABLE BOARD, $1.50 PER WEEK. | TOTAL EXPENSES, $100 TO $125 PER YEAR.

Competent Teachers in Each Department. Tuition Only $6.00 Per Term. No Incidental Fee.
SATISFACTION GUARANTEED.
For Catalogue, address the Principal.

ORGANS AND PIANOS.

BEATTY
ORGANS & PIANOS.
Organs, Church, Chapel and Parlor, $30 to $1,000, 2 to 32 Stops. Pianofortes, Grand, Square & Upright, $125 to $1,600. Sent on trial warranted. Illustrated Catalogue with Steel-Plate FREE. Address or call on Daniel F. Beatty, Washington, N. J.

BEATTY
CABINET ORGANS.
CHURCH, CHAPEL AND PARLOR.
BEATTY PIANOFORTES,
GRAND SQUARE AND UPRIGHT.
Best and Sweetest-Toned Instrument in the World. ORGANS $30, $40, $50, to $1,000, 2 to 32 Stops. PIANOS, $125 up to $1,600. Every instrument fully Warranted. Sent on trial. Beautiful Illustrated Catalogue and Steel-Plate Engraving free. Those desiring to buy are requested to visit my factory here, and select the instrument in person. Address or call on Daniel F. Beatty, Washington, N. J.

ORGANS 14 Stops, 4 Sets Reeds, ONLY $65. PIANOS, $125 up. Paper free. Address Daniel F. Beatty, Washington, N. J.

BEATTY
ORGANS & PIANOS.
Organs, Church, Chapel and Parlor, $30 to $1,000, 2 to 32 Stops. Pianofortes, Grand, Square & Upright, $125 to $1,000. Sent on trial warranted. Illustrated Catalogue with Steel-Plate FREE. Address or call on Daniel F. Beatty, Washington, N. J.

ORGANS AND PIANOS.

BEATTY CABINET ORGANS.
CHURCH, CHAPEL, AND PARLOR.
BEATTY PIANOFORTES,
GRAND SQUARE AND UPRIGHT.
Best and Sweetest-Toned Instrument in the World. **ORGANS** $30, $40, $50, to $1,000, 2 to 32 Stops. **PIANOS**, $125 up to $1,600. Every instrument **fully Warranted**. Sent on trial. Beautiful Illustrated Catalogue and **Steel-Plate Engraving free**. Those desiring to buy are requested to visit my factory here, and select the instrument in person. Address or call on Daniel F. Beatty, Washington, N. J.

ORGANS 14 Stops, 4 Sets Reeds, ONLY $65. PIANOS, $125 up. Paper free. Address Daniel F. Beatty, Washington, N. J.

BEATTY CABINET ORGANS.
CHURCH, CHAPEL AND PARLOR.
BEATTY PIANOFORTES,
GRAND SQUARE AND UPRIGHT.
Best and Sweetest-Toned Instrument in the World. **ORGANS** $30, $40, $50, to $1,000, 2 to 32 Stops. **PIANOS**, $125 up to $1,600. Every instrument **fully Warranted**. Sent on trial. Beautiful Illustrated Catalogue and **Steel-Plate Engraving free**. Those desiring to buy are requested to visit my factory here, and select the instrument in person. Address or call on Daniel F. Beatty, Washington, N. J.

ORGANS 14 Stops, 4 Sets Reeds, ONLY $65. PIANOS, $125 up. Paper free. Address Daniel F. Beatty, Washington, N. J.

ORGANS AND PIANOS.

BEATTY

ORGANS & PIANOS.

Organs. Church, Chapel and Parlor, $30 to $1,000, 2 to 32 Stops. Pianofortes, Grand, Square & Upright, $125 to $1,600. Sent on trial warranted. Illustrated Catalogue with Steel-Plate FREE. Address or call on Daniel F. Beatty, Washington, N. J.

ORGANS 14 Stops, 4 Sets Reeds, ONLY $65. PIANOS, $125 up. Paper free. Address Daniel F. Beatty, Washington, N. J.

BEATTY

ORGANS & PIANOS.

Organs. Church, Chapel and Parlor, $30 to $1,000, 2 to 32 Stops. Pianofortes, Grand, Square & Upright, $125 to $1,600. Sent on trial warranted. Illustrated Catalogue with Steel-Plate FREE. Address or call on Daniel F. Beatty, Washington, N. J.

BEATTY

CABINET ORGANS.

CHURCH, CHAPEL AND PARLOR.
BEATTY PIANOFORTES,
GRAND SQUARE AND UPRIGHT.
Best and Sweetest-Toned Instrument in the World.
ORGANS $30, $40, $50, to $1,000, 2 to 32 Stops. PIANOS, $125 up to $1,600. Every instrument fully Warranted. Sent on trial. Beautiful Illustrated Catalogue and Steel-Plate Engraving free. Those desiring to buy are requested to visit my factory here, and select the instrument in person.
Address or call on Daniel F. Beatty, Washington, N. J.

www.ingramcontent.com/pod-product-compliance
Lightning Source LLC
Chambersburg PA
CBHW032108220426
43664CB00008B/1172